EXCEL® STUDENT LABORATORY MANUAL AND WORKBOOK

JOHANNA HALSEY

Dutchess Community College

ELLENA REDA

Dutchess Community College

to accompany

ELEMENTARY STATISTICS

NINTH EDITION

and

ELEMENTARY STATISTICS USING EXCEL®

SECOND EDITION

Mario F. Triola

Dutchess Community College

PEARSON

Addison Wesley

Boston   San Francisco   New York
London   Toronto   Sydney   Tokyo   Singapore   Madrid
Mexico City   Munich   Paris   Cape Town   Hong Kong   Montreal

PEARSON

Addison
Wesley

Preface

Purpose of the Manual

This manual contains step-by-step instructions to help you familiarize yourself with the spreadsheet program Excel®. Our primary purpose in creating the instructions is to help you become proficient with the features of Excel that lend support to working with data in your statistics class.

We know that it is impossible to cover every possible option in using the program, so we have chosen the techniques that have worked well for us and our own students. There are usually at least two ways to produce the same results. Our hope is that providing you with a solid set of step by step instructions, you will become comfortable enough with the program to begin to experiment on your own, and share your discoveries with other students in your class.

Layout of the Manual

Other than Chapter 1, this manual follows *Elementary Statistics,* 9th Edition section by section. Almost all of the exercises worked through in the tutorial instructions are taken directly from that particular section in your text. At the end of each section you will find reference to several exercises which will give you an opportunity to practice the technology skills introduced within that section. Our hope is that you will immediately employ the features you learn in Excel to help you with the exercises and projects that are presented in that section of your textbook. You will find that utilizing the technology to work on many exercises in the book will afford you the essential practice necessary to become proficient with the program.

Using Technology Wisely

Any software package has its own learning curve. You should expect it to take a certain investment of time and energy and regular practice to become comfortable with using Excel. The more regularly you commit to using the ideas presented in this manual, the more proficient and adept you will become with using this program when and where appropriate.

While there are many, many places that Excel can, and should be integrated into the course material, you also can benefit from doing some of the work without using any technology. To truly understand some concepts, you need to perform at least some of the computations by hand. Once you have a core understanding of an idea, the technology affords you a way to find answers quickly and accurately.

Technology Notes

The instructions contained in this manual are written for a PC. Keystrokes may vary for those using a Mac. Mac users should note that Ctrl + click has the same functionality as a right click for PC users and a single click has the same functionality as a left click.

Early in the manual, you will be asked to load the Data Desk®/XL (DDXL) Add-In that accompanies your textbook. This Add-In supplements Excel, providing additional statistical tools not included in Excel. For example you will use DDXL to construct boxplots, confidence intervals and to perform hypothesis tests.

You can find the data sets from Appendix B of your textbook on the CD-ROM that accompanies your text. You can also download these data sets from the Internet at http://www.aw.com/triola.

Final Notes

We feel that the benefits of using Excel in a statistics course are vast. Many companies look for employees who are proficient with using spreadsheets. By learning how you can use Excel to support your work in statistics, you will simultaneously be developing a skill that is highly valued in the business world. Our hope is that this manual provides you with a relatively painless entry into the world of spreadsheets! We hope you enjoy your learning journey.

Johanna Halsey

Ellena Reda

CONTENTS

CHAPTER 1: GETTING STARTED WITH MICROSOFT EXCEL

SECTION 1-1: INTRODUCTION

One of the most valuable computer programs used in business today is the spreadsheet. Spreadsheets are used to organize and analyze data, to perform calculations and to show relationships in data through various types of charts and graphs. Many computers come preloaded with Microsoft Office®. Excel is part of the Microsoft Office Suite. It is a popular spreadsheet program and can be used by all skill levels.

The purpose of this chapter is to provide you, the student, with an introduction to spreadsheets and to prepare you to use Excel in the study of statistics. The best way to learn the basics is to dive in. As you explore Excel you will notice that there are often several ways to perform the same task. This manual will highlight only one or two of those ways. However that should not prevent you from trying other ways or using a method you already are familiar with.

SECTION 1-2: THE BASICS

You may open the Excel program one of two ways:

1)   double click on the **Excel icon** found on the desktop screen
OR
2)   from the **Start** menu – highlight **Programs** – highlight **Microsoft Excel** -then click on the left mouse
button (Mac users just click).

When you start Excel, a blank worksheet appears. This worksheet is the document that Excel uses for storing and manipulating data.

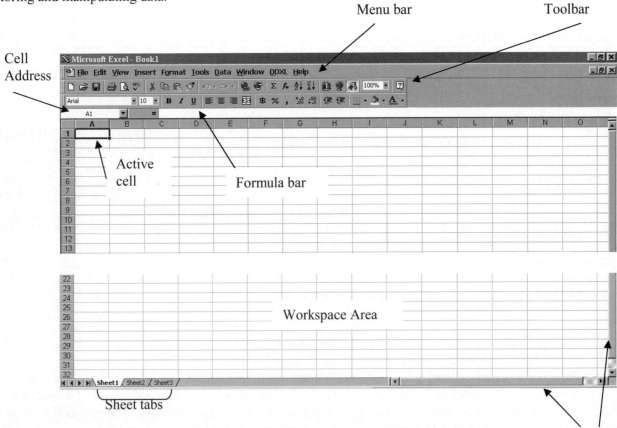

The following are some **basic terms** that you should be familiar with. Locate each of these on your Excel screen:

Toolbar – An area of the Excel screen containing a series of icon buttons used to access commands and other features. To find out what each toolbar icon does, place the mouse pointer over the button without clicking and its name will appear.

Menu bar – Groups of command choices. To view those choices click on one of the commands and a menu of commands in that group will drop down.

Worksheet area – The grid of rows and columns into which you enter text, numbers and formulas.

Cell – located at the intersection of a row and a column. Information is inserted into a cell by clicking on cell and entering the information directly.

Cell address – Location of a cell based on the intersection of a row and a column. In a cell address the column is always listed first and the row second so that A1 means column A row 1.

Active cell – The worksheet cell receiving the information you type. The active cell is surrounded by a thick border. The address of the active cell is displayed above the worksheet on the left.

Formula bar – Area near the top of the Excel screen where you enter and edit data.

Scroll bars – allow you to display parts of the worksheet that are currently off screen such as row 35 or column R.

Sheet tabs – Identify the names of individual worksheets.

SECTION 1-3: ENTERING AND EDITING DATA INTO EXCEL

When an Excel worksheet is first opened, the cell A1 is automatically the active cell. Notice that A1 is surrounded by a dark black box. This indicates that it is the **active cell**. Note that A1 is also shown in the **cell address** box as well.

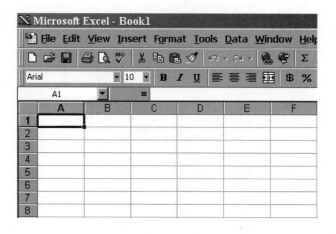

If you press a key by mistake, clear out information you may have wanted or find the screen isn't doing quite what you expect it to do try clicking the **Undo button** located on the toolbar. It looks like an arrow looping to the left.

THE FORMULA BAR

The formula bar is located in the fourth row of your Excel worksheet, to the right of the cell address box. The first window on the formula bar shown below indicates the cell address of the active cell. The **red X** is used when we wish to delete information we have typed into the active cell. The **green check mark** can be clicked to indicate that the data or formula you have entered into the active cell is acceptable.

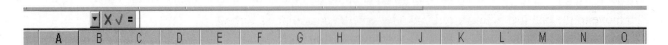

There are three types of information that may be entered into a cell:

- Text

- Numbers

- Formulas

ENTERING TEXT AND NUMBERS

The following exercise will give you some practice in entering both text and numbers into a worksheet.

1) Position the mouse pointer on cell C1 and click on the left mouse button. This makes cell C1 the active cell.

2) Type "ANNUAL SALES REPORT" (without the quotation marks) in cell C1 and press **Enter.** Notice that the active cell is now C2.

3) Activate cell A3 by clicking on that cell.

4) Type "REGION" in cell A3. Press the **Tab** key or the **right arrow** key to move to cell B3.

5) Similarly enter

"QRTR 1" in cell B3	"TOTAL" in cell F3
"QRTR 2" in cell C3	"EAST" in cell A5
"QRTR 3" in cell D3	"SOUTH" in cell A6
"QRTR 4" in cell E3	"WEST" in cell A7

6) To complete the worksheet shown below, begin by activating cell B5 and typing the data shown.

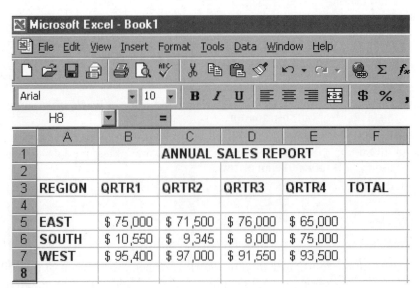

Note:

To move to the cell just below a cell you have entered data in press **Enter.**

To move to the right of a cell you have just entered data in press **Tab.**

FORMATTING CELLS

The information that you have entered into the Excel spreadsheet represents the total sales figures. These should be represented as dollar amounts, although this may not be apparent when you first enter the data.

The following shows the formatting icons found in your Excel worksheet.

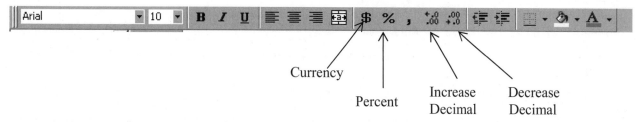

Currency

Percent

Increase
Decimal

Decrease
Decimal

The **increase decimal or decrease decimal** icons both allow us to determine the number of values that will be displayed to the right of the **decimal.**

To Format Cells

There are two different ways to change the values you have entered so that they represent dollar amounts:

Method 1:

1) Click on the **B** at the top of the second column. The entire column is now highlighted.

2) Click on the **currency** icon ($) found on the formatting tool bar.

3) All data in that column should now contain a dollar sign in front of it.

Method 2:

1) Select the cells you wish to format.

2) Click on **Format** from the Menu Bar**,** highlight **Cells** and click.

3) This will open a **Format Cells** dialog box. This dialog box presents a number of options to you, that include the ability to choose the type of number and the number of decimal places you wish displayed.

4) Try using this method to change all of your data in your worksheet to dollar amounts at the same time.

SAVING YOUR WORK

Once you have entered data into an Excel spreadsheet you will want to save your work. This can be done by either clicking the **Save** icon on the toolbar (it looks like a floppy disk) or by clicking on **File** in the menu bar and choosing the **Save** command.

- A dialog box will appear similar to the one you see on the right.

- Choose **Drive A** to save the information to a **floppy disk**.

- Choose **C** to save information to your **hard drive.**

- Enter a **file name** that will accurately indicate what the file contains and then click on **Save**.

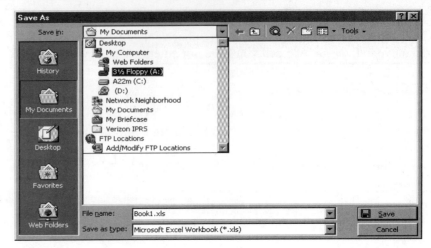

Note:
It is a good idea to follow the wise old adage of "save and save often." When working on a spreadsheet, it is always a good idea to click on the **Save** icon periodically.

EDITING INFORMATION

To empty the contents of a cell, we have already mentioned using the **red X** found on the formula bar. Information that has not been entered can be removed by using the backspace key. Once you have entered data, it can be removed by simply activating the cell which contains the information you wish to remove and pressing the delete key.

After data has been entered you can edit the information in a cell by activating that cell (click on it). The information in that cell is now displayed in the formula bar. Move your cursor to the entry you wish to modify or change. The cursor will turn into what looks like the capital letter I, commonly referred to as an I-beam. Place the I-beam at the point you wish to make changes, left click and proceed from there.

SELECT A RANGE OF CELLS

We often need to select more than one cell at a time. A group of selected cells is called a **Range** of cells. To select more than one cell at a time

1) Click on a cell (in this example we are using cell B3) and hold the left mouse button down.

2) With the cursor in the middle of the cell move down to cell B8.

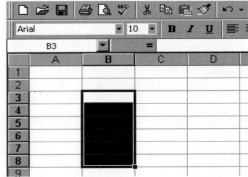

3) Release the left mouse button. The cells B3 through B8 should now be highlighted.

We refer to this **range of cells** as **B3:B8**, using a colon to separate the first cell in the range from the last cell.

DROPPING AND DRAGGING

To easily move or copy a range of cells from your worksheet we can use a shortcut method known as **drop and drag**.

To move a range of cells

1) Select the cells using the method previously outlined

2) Position the cursor anywhere on the border of the range of cells you have highlighted.

3) Hold the left mouse key down.

4) Drag the range of cells to their new location.

5) Release the mouse button.

To copy a range of cells

1) Select the cells as you did above, release the mouse

2) Position the cursor anywhere on the border of the range of cells you have highlighted.

3) Hold the left mouse key and the **CTRL** key down at the same time.

4) Move to data to the location into which you wish it to be copied.

5) Release the mouse key, then the **CTRL** key. (The order in which you release the keys is important).

Note:
You can **Undo Drop and Drag** by locating this command in the **Edit** menu.

OPENING FILES IN EXCEL

As you work through this manual and on exercises in your textbook, you will be asked to open files you have saved to a floppy disk or the hard drive or use data sets found on the CD-ROM Data Disk that accompanied your Statistics textbook. These data sets are the same as the data found in Appendix B of your text.

To use the data sets on the CD-ROM
1) Open Excel.

2) Place the CD into the **CD-ROM drive** on your computer. This is often drive D or E.

3) Click on **File**, found on the menu bar, highlight **Open** and click.

4) A dialog box similar to the one shown on the next page will appear. You will need to choose the appropriate location for the files you wish to open.
   a) Choose **Drive A** if the information is on a **floppy disk**.
   b) Choose **C** for information on the hard drive.
   c) For information stored on a CD choose **D** if this is the **CD-ROM drive**.

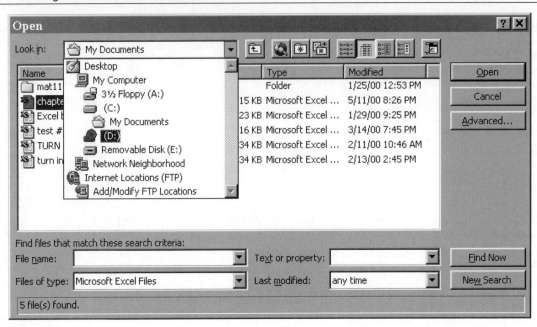

5) A second dialog box opens. This dialog box shows two files "DataSets" and "Software." Double click on **DataSets**.

6) This presents another dialog box as shown below. For a list of the files for Excel double click on the **Excel folder.** Use the scroll bar on the right of the dialog box to view the complete list of data files.

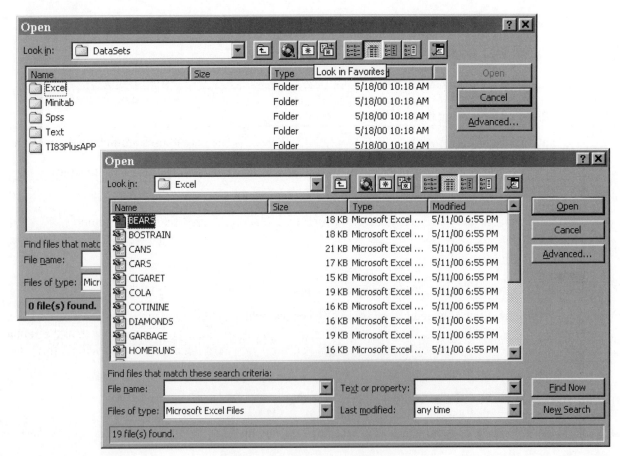

7) Identify the file you are looking for by file name. Click on the **file name**.

8) Click **Open**.

The same process is used when opening a file that contains data that you may save saved to a floppy disk or to your hard drive.

SECTION 1-4: UNDERSTANDING AND USING FORMULAS:

To analyze data in Excel it is frequently necessary to perform calculations using formulas. When entering a formula in Excel we can either use the actual value found within a cell or the cell address. When you type formulas in Excel the software program requires that you type an equal sign (=) at the start of your formula. This identifies the entry as a formula. As you create a formula, it is displayed in the formula bar. The numerical results are displayed in the cell itself. After you have typed in the formula and presses the Enter key, Excel automatically performs the calculation. If you change a number stored in a cell address used in the formula, Excel automatically recalculates the results of that formula.

Operators & Order of Operation

The formulas used in Excel make use of basic arithmetic operations. The symbols that are used for these **common operators** are:

Addition	+	Subtraction	—
Multiplication	*	Division	/
Exponents	^		

Excel also follows the basic **rules for order of operation** that we are all familiar with. Therefore it is important that when you input a formula you are very specific in the way the information is typed.

$\dfrac{2+3(2)^5}{5}$ would be entered as follows $(2 + 3 * 2 \wedge 5)/5$ in Excel. The parentheses around the expression $(2 + 3 * 2 \wedge 5)$ are important because they indicate that $(2 + 3 * 2 \wedge 5)$ is the numerator and the entire expression need to be divided by 5.

Remember that formulas and equations generally contain a cell address rather than actual numbers.

Entering a Formula

1) **Select the cell** in which a formula is to be entered.

2) Type an = **(equal sign)** followed by the formula. The formula should be surrounded by a set of parentheses. It is often easier to use the cell address within any formulas you write rather than the actual number although you can use either one. Using a cell address is advantageous when copying a formula to other cells.

3) After typing in the formula press **Enter**.

4) Open the file you saved when working in the previous section on text and numbers.

5) To find the total sales for the "East Region" begin by clicking on cell F5, the cell in which we want our answer displayed.

6) **Type** the formula = (B5+C5 +D5+E5).

7) Press **Enter**.

8) Repeat to find the totals of each row. Compare your answers with those below.

	A	B	C	D	E	F
1			ANNUAL SALES REPORT			
2						
3	REGION	QRTR1	QRTR2	QRTR3	QRTR4	TOTAL
4						
5	EAST	$ 75,000	$ 71,500	$ 76,000	$ 65,000	$ 287,500
6	SOUTH	$ 10,550	$ 9,345	$ 8,000	$ 7,500	$ 35,395
7	WEST	$ 95,400	$ 97,000	$ 91,550	$ 93,500	$ 377,450
8						

(Microsoft Excel - exercise 1; formula bar for F5 shows =(B5+C5+D5+E5); Arial 10)

Notice that F5 has a black border around it indicating that it is the active cell. Also notice that the formula used to find the total in F5 is displayed in the formula bar.

Note:

Typing in each cell address to be added together in each of the columns above works well if there is a small number of cell addresses to be entered. If we had 50 data entries to add together in column B we would not want to type = (B1 + B2 + B3 + …. + B50).

To save time we can enter the same information by typing in the cell address for range of cells, in this case type = SUM (B1:B50).

Copying a Formula

In our previous problems, you probably retyped the formulas to find TOTAL in the appropriate cells. However, it is not necessary to re-type similar formulas. It is possible to copy an existing formula into other cells.

Method 1: (useful if you are copying the same formula to a series of cells)

1) Click on the cell that already contains the formula you want to copy.

2) Place your mouse on the lower right hand corner of the highlighted cell. When your cursor changes to a cross (commonly referred to as the **fill handle**), click and hold the left mouse button and drag the box to cover the cells where you wish to copy the formula.

3) When you release the mouse button the formula will be copied and adjusted for these cells. This can be seen in the illustration on the following page.

F5	▼	=	=(B5+C5+D5+E5)

	A	B	C	D	E	F
1			ANNUAL SALES REPORT			
2						
3	REGION	QRTR1	QRTR2	QRTR3	QRTR4	TOTAL
4						
5	EAST	$ 75,000	$ 71,500	$ 76,000	$ 65,000	$ 287,500
6	SOUTH	$ 10,550	$ 9,345	$ 8,000	$ 7,500	
7	WEST	$ 95,400	$ 97,000	$ 91,550	$ 93,500	
8						
9						

Notice that the mouse pointer changes to a cross

Method 2: (useful if you are only copying one piece of information to another cell)

1) Click on the cell that already contains the formula you want to copy.

2) Click on the **copy** icon found on the tool bar (or use **Ctrl + C**).

3) Click on the new cell into which you wish to copy the formula.

4) Choose the **paste** icon found on the toolbar. (Or use **Ctrl + V**).

Try both methods on the worksheet you have created to determine which works best for you.

SECTION 1- 5: RELATIVE AND ABSOLUTE REFERENCE

Cell references can be **relative** or **absolute.** The cell references we have used so far are all **relative references** and when these references are copied to a new location they change to reflect their new position. In the preceding problem the formula from cell F5 was = (B5 + C5 + D5 + E5). When this formula was copied to cell F6 the formula changed to = (B6 + C6 + D6 +E6) reflecting a new relative position one row below where the original information was entered. This relative address feature makes it easy for us to copy a formula by entering it once in a cell and then copying its contents to other cells.

An **absolute reference** does not automatically adjust when moved to another cell and is used when it is necessary to retain the value in a specific cell address when copying a formula. In an absolute reference both values in the cell address are preceded by a $. For example, the formula = ($B$5 + $C$5 + $D$5 + $E$5) will remain unchanged regardless of the cell to which it is copied. The dollar sign does not signify currency but rather is used to identify that the cell is an absolute reference.

Formulas can contain both relative and absolute cell references. For example, suppose I wished to determine what percentage of the total sales came from each region (East, South and West) in the problem we have been working with so far. I would begin by totaling the amount of sales found in column F. This information can now be found in F8 as seen below. To determine the percentage of sales for the East region I would need to divide the sales for the East region by the total sales OR F5/$F$8 and enter this formula in cell G5. The use of an absolute reference will allow us to copy this formula down column G. The top value will adjust to reference the cell we are in while the bottom value (the absolute reference) will remain constant, as we would want it to.

	A	B	C	D	E	F	G	H
1			ANNUAL SALES REPORT					
2								
3	REGION	QRTR1	QRTR2	QRTR3	QRTR4	TOTAL		
4								
5	EAST	$ 75,000	$ 71,500	$ 76,000	$ 65,000	$ 287,500	=(F5/$F$8)	
6	SOUTH	$ 10,550	$ 9,345	$ 8,000	$ 7,500	$ 35,395		
7	WEST	$ 95,400	$ 97,000	$ 91,550	$ 93,500	$ 377,450		
8						$700,345.00		
9								

SECTION 1-6: MODIFYING YOUR WORKBOOK

INSERTING AND DELETING ROWS/COLUMNS

Sometimes you will want to insert or delete columns or rows from your worksheet. If you want to create additional space in the middle of a worksheet you can insert a column or a row that will run the entire length or width of the worksheet. If you have an entire row or column that is no longer necessary you can delete the entire column or row.

To Insert a Row (or Column)

1) Highlight the row (or column) by right clicking on the number at the start of the row (or letter at the head of the column).

2) A dialog box should open. Choose **INSERT**. The new row will be inserted *above* the selected row. A new column will be inserted to the *left* of the selected column.

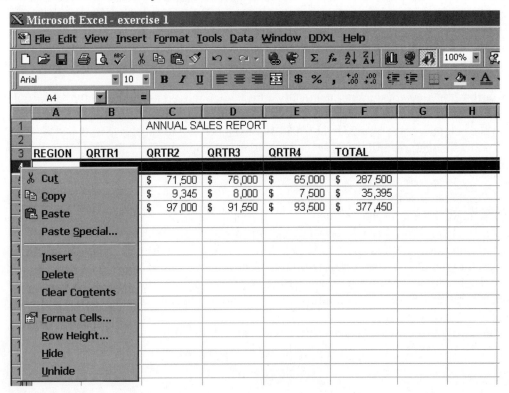

To Delete a Row (or Column)

1) Highlight the row (or column) by right clicking on the number at the start of the row (or letter at the head of the column).

2) As seen on the preceding page - a dialog box should open. Choose **DELETE**. The old row (or column) is removed from the worksheet and is replaced by the data in the adjoining row (or column).

Note:
Pressing the **Delete** key does not delete the selected row or column. It clears all data from the selection without moving in replacement data. Click a cell outside of the selected row (or column) to deselect it.

CHANGING COLUMN WIDTH AND ROW HEIGHT

Often we are in a position where we wish to change the width of a column. Text is often cut off because the column is not wide enough to display all that we have entered into the cell. If a cell can't display an entire number or date, the cell may fill with ####### or display a value in scientific notation. (Try entering a 12 digit number into a cell.)

To Adjust the Column Width

1) Position the mouse pointer on the right border of the lettered heading at the top of the column you wish to adjust. The mouse pointer should change to a black cross with an arrow head at each end of the horizontal line.

2) Press and hold down the left mouse button, dragging the right side of the column to increase or decrease the column width.

3) Move the mouse back and forth. Release the mouse button when you have a column the width you like.

To Adjust the Row Height

1) Position the mouse pointer on the lower border of the numbered row whose size you wish to adjust. The mouse pointer should change to a black cross with an arrowhead at each end of the horizontal line.

2) Press and hold down the left mouse button, dragging the border to increase or decrease the row height.

3) Move the mouse back and forth. Release the mouse button when you have a row at the height you like.

To Add Worksheets to a Workbook

When you open a new workbook in Excel you will see that there are three worksheets available to you. This gives you the ability to do three separate problems or variations of a problem all within one workbook. While only three worksheets are presented, it is possible to have up to sixteen worksheets within one workbook.

1) Click on **Insert** on the menu Bar,

2) Highlight **Worksheet**, and then click.

You will notice an additional worksheet tab in the bottom area of the screen.

To Rename a Worksheet

Initially the worksheets in Excel are labeled "Sheet 1" "Sheet 2" and "Sheet 3." To help keep track of information found in the various worksheets in your workbook, it is often useful to rename your worksheets.

1) Right click on the worksheet tab that you would like to rename

2) Highlight **Rename** and click. The sheet tab should now be highlighted.

3) Begin typing the new name for this worksheet.

4) Press **Enter** when you have finished.

INSERTING A COMMENT

There are many instances when it is important to annotate work done in Excel by attaching a note to a cell. This is done by adding comments that can be viewed when you rest the cursor over that cell.

To enter a comment into an Excel worksheet:

1) Click the cell to which you want to add the comment.

2) Click on the **Insert** menu.

3) Highlight **Comment**, the click.

4) In the box, type the text of your comment.

5) When you finish typing the text, click outside the comment box.

6) A triangle will appear in the upper right hand corner of the cell that contains a comment.

7) To view the comment, move the cursor over the cell that contains the note.

8) The comment will appear.

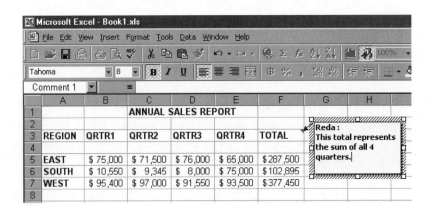

To Show, Edit or Remove a Comment:

To make a comment **visible** at all times:

1) Right click on the cell that contains the comment.

2) Highlight **Show Comment,** and then click.

To **edit** a comment:

1) Right click on the cell that contains the comment.

2) Highlight **Edit Comment**, and then click.

To **remove** a comment:

1) Right click on the cell that contains the comment.

2) Highlight **Delete Comment,** and then click.

SECTION 1- 7: PRINTING YOUR EXCEL WORK

There are many occasions where you will want to print a worksheet or workbook you have created in Excel. While it is possible to print all of the sheets in a workbook in one operation it is highly recommended that you print each worksheet separately. It is *always recommended* that you use the **Print Preview** before printing anything. This will allow you to catch and correct mistakes before you print a page.

1) To preview your worksheet before you print it, click on **File** from the Menu Bar, highlight **Print Preview** and click. This will give you an opportunity to make sure all of your work is presented within the printable page.

2) Click on **Close** once you have previewed your worksheet.

3) To print click on **File,** highlight **Print** and click. A Print dialog box will appear and should be similar to the one shown below. In it you will see the name of the printer being used (yours) as well as other options.

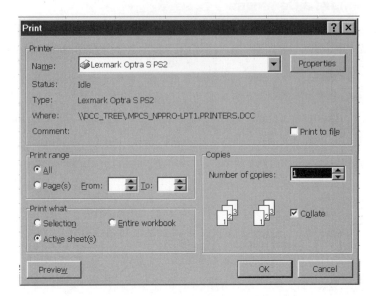

4) You can also customize your worksheet before printing. Click on **File**, highlight **Page Setup** and click.

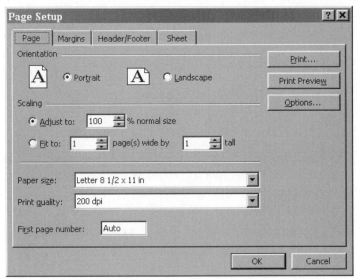

- **Page Tab** – allows you to choose the orientation of the printed page, either vertically (Portrait) or horizontally (Landscape). Landscape is useful for worksheets that have a greater width than they do length.

- **Margin Tab** – allows you to adjust the margin of the printed page.

- **Header/Footer Tab** – gives you the opportunity to include headers or footers on the printed page.

- **Sheet Tab** – the Print area is the most useful option on this tab.

- **Print area** - allows you to choose whether or not to include gridlines and row and column headings in the printout of your worksheet. It also gives you the opportunity to select a particular range to print from your worksheet. Click in the box to the right of Print area; highlight the range of cells you wish to print. You can also enter the information by typing in the range of cells.

Once you have completed making your choices click **OK**.

SECTION 1- 8: GETTING HELP WHILE USING EXCEL

Excel comes with a complete on-line Help feature designed to give assistance when you are having difficulty with a topic. You can access the Help system by selecting an option from the **HELP** Menu located at the top of the screen. Choose either Microsoft Excel Help or Contents and Index.

- **Microsoft Excel Help** gives you the opportunity to type in a question and search for an answer.
- **Contents and Index**:
  Contents is like the table of contents in a book providing an overview of major categories.
  Index is like the index in the back of a book providing an alphabetical list of the help that is available.

TO PRACTICE THESE SKILLS

It is important to practice those technology skills introduced in this chapter before moving on. To help you do this work through the following problem in Excel.

Temperature Conversions

The formula for converting degrees Fahrenheit to degrees Celsius is $C = \dfrac{5}{9}(F - 32)$. Use Excel to set up a spread sheet to do these conversions given a set of temperatures.

d) Type "Degrees Fahrenheit" in Cell A1.

e) Type "Degrees Celsius" in Cell B1.

f) In cells A2 through A11 enter the following temperatures recorded in degrees Fahrenheit:

$-10^{\circ}, 0^{\circ}, 10^{\circ}, 32^{\circ}, 45^{\circ}, 50^{\circ}, 68^{\circ}, 75^{\circ}, 83^{\circ}, 95^{\circ}.$

g) In cell B2 enter the formula to convert from degrees Fahrenheit to degrees Celsius using an appropriate cell address.

h) Copy this formula through to cell B11.

i) Format the values in column B correct to 2 decimal places.

j) Rename your worksheet "Temperature Conversion."

k) Print out your worksheet.

CHAPTER 2: DESCRIBING, EXPLORING AND COMPARING DATA

SECTION 2-1: OVERVIEW

In this chapter, we will use the capabilities of Excel to help us look more carefully at sets of data. We can do this by re-organizing the data, creating pictures, or by creating summary statistics. The sections that follow take you through step by step directions on how to create frequency distributions and histograms, as well as other types of visual models. We will also utilize the descriptive statistics capabilities of Excel to create representative values for the data set.

ADD-IN: ANALYSIS TOOLPAK

Before you begin your work in this chapter, make sure that you have the **Analysis ToolPak** loaded on your machine. This is an Add-In in Excel. You may need to access your Excel software disk to add this feature.

To see if the ToolPak has already been loaded on your machine, click on **Tools** in the menu bar, and see if **Data Analysis** is listed. If not, follow the steps below:

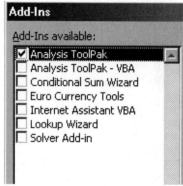

1) Click on **Tools**, and select **Add-Ins**.

2) In the **Add-Ins** dialog box, check **Analysis Tool-Pak**.

3) Click on **OK**.

The ToolPak will be loaded, and when you click on **Tools** you should now see **Data Analysis** listed at the bottom of the menu.

SECTION 2-2: FREQUENCY DISTRIBUTIONS

In this section, we will use the data from Data Set 6 in Appendix B. Load this data into a new worksheet. This data can also be found on the CD-ROM data disk that accompanies your textbook. Open the file named: COTININE.

You should get in the habit of preserving your original data in one of the sheets in your workbook. This way, you can always easily retrieve it if necessary. To begin work, once you have opened a file containing data, or input data directly, you should copy the original data to a new worksheet in that workbook.

1) After loading the original data from your CD, or typing the data in from Appendix B, double click on the tab at the bottom of the worksheet so that "Sheet 1" is highlighted. Type in "Original Data."

2) If you loaded the data from your CD, your data appears in columns A, B and C. Select the columns A through C by clicking on the "A" and holding your mouse down as you pull your cursor over to "C." (If you typed the data in manually, select the columns containing your data. If you left blank columns in between data sets, you can also select them.) Let your mouse key up. The columns with your data should now be highlighted. Copy these columns by selecting **Edit** from your menu bar, and then selecting **Copy**. You should see a dotted box around your data.

3) At the bottom of your worksheet, click on Sheet 2. Position your cursor at the top of column A and click. This column should now be selected.

4) Click on **Edit** in your menu bar, and then select **Paste**. Your data should be copied into Sheet 2.

5) Try to get in the habit of naming the different sheets in your workbook so that it is clear what is contained in each sheet. Since we will be creating a frequency distribution from part of the data, you may want to rename your "Sheet 2" with a name like "Frequency."

We will use this data to construct the frequency distribution found in Table 2-2 in your book, which summarizes the measured cotinine levels of the 40 smokers listed in Table 2-1.

CREATING A FREQUENCY DISTRIBUTION

In order to create a frequency distribution, we need to indicate what **upper class limits** we want to use. Excel refers to these upper class limits as "bins."   Before using Excel, you need to determine how many classes you want, what your class width will be, and what your lower and upper class limits will be for the particular data set.

If we want to construct a frequency distribution with 5 classes, class width of 100, starting with the value 0, we should enter the **upper class limits** of 99, 199, 299, 399 and 499 into a column. We will name this column "Bin" to help familiarize ourselves with the terminology that is programmed into Excel.

1) In a new worksheet, load the data from Data Set 6, or if the data is not available in electronic format, type the data from Table 2-1 in your book in 3 columns titled **Smoker, ETS, and NOETS.**

2) In a blank column several columns to the left of the data, type the name "Bins" in the first cell of your selected column.

3) Type the values 99, 199, 299, 399, 499 into your selected column, starting directly in the cell beneath the column heading. (If your title "Bins" was in cell G1, you would enter the values given in cells G2 through G6.)

4) Click on **Tools** and select **Data Analysis**. (If necessary, go back to the instructions in Section 2-1 to learn how to add this feature to your machine.)

5) Double click on **Histogram** (or select **Histogram** and click on **OK**). You will see a dialog box similar to the following. To input the values shown, follow the directions below.

a) You need to tell Excel where the input and Bin values are located. Since we want the frequency distribution of Cotinine Levels of Smokers, for the "Input Range," we need to tell Excel where this data can be found. You can either type the cell range in the box with a colon separating the first and last cell (for example, type **A2:A41** if your data can be found in these cells) **OR** select the cells where this data is located in your worksheet. (Refer back to Chapter 1 if you need to review how to select a range of cells.) You may want to first click on the "collapse" icon on the right hand side of your "Input Range" box. This

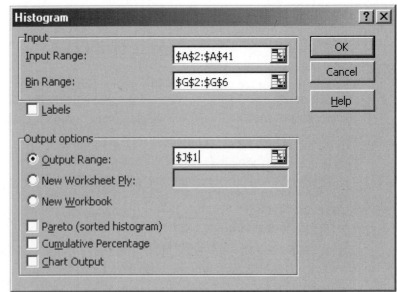

will collapse the dialog box, and allow you to move freely around your worksheet. Once you have selected your input, click on the "expand" icon to go back to the dialog box.

b) In the **Bin Range** box, either type in the range of cells where the bin values are located with a colon in between cell names, or select these cells in your worksheet.

c) To position your output in the same worksheet, click in front of **Output Range**, then click inside the entry box, and type the cell location where you want your data to begin. From the dialog box above, Excel will position the output for the frequency distribution starting in cell J1. Once you have clicked inside the entry box, you could also select the cell where you want your output positioned by clicking in a specific cell in your worksheet. If you are going to overwrite data that already exists in your worksheet, a warning dialog box will appear.

	J	K
	Bin	Frequency
	99	11
	199	12
	299	14
	399	1
	499	2
More		0

d) To position your output in a separate worksheet, click in front of **New Worksheet Ply**, and type in a meaningful name such as Histogram.

e) Click on **OK**. You should now see a frequency distribution for your data.

Note:
You should remember to interpret the frequencies as the number of values that are less than or equal to the upper class limits that you typed into your bins, but greater than the previous upper class limit.

Looking at the frequency distribution for the Distribution of Cotinine Levels of Smokers, you should interpret that there are 12 ratings between 100 and 199 (less than or equal to the bin value 199, but greater than the previous bin value 99).

Modifying the Frequency Distribution

1) Notice that when Excel created the frequency distribution, there is an extra row labeled "More." To remove this extra row, highlight only the two cells in the frequency distribution that you wish to remove. Click on **Edit**, highlight and click on **Delete,** click in the bubble by **Shift Cells Up,** and then click on **OK.**

2) To rename the columns of the frequency distribution, click on the name at the top of the column, and type in the new name you would like to use. For this example, rather than use the word "Bins", it makes more sense to type in what the values represent: "Cotinine Levels of Smokers". This name would extend over a larger region than the original column width. To rectify this, after you type in the heading, click on another cell, and then re-click on the cell containing your heading. With this cell selected, click on **Format,** and then click on **Cells.** In the dialog box that appears, click on **Alignment**, and click in the box in front of "Wrap Text." Then click on **OK**.

3) You should also consider changing the initial bin values to show the actual classes, or indicate in your heading that the values represent the Upper Limits for your classes. Keep in mind, to create the original frequency distribution, Excel needs the bin values (upper class limits). Once the table is created, you can replace the bin values in the table with the actual classes, or the class midpoints. A final form of the frequency distribution might look like the following:

J	K
Cotinine Levels of Smokers	Frequency
0 - 99	11
100 - 199	12
200 - 299	14
300 - 399	1
400 - 499	2

CREATING A RELATIVE FREQUENCY DISTRIBUTION

To create a relative frequency distribution, we need to add a column for relative frequencies to our frequency distribution. The relative frequency for a particular class will be equal to the number of values in that class divided by the total number of values in the data set. To set up this column in the frequency distribution follow the steps below.

1) In a cell under the entries in the first column of your frequency distribution, type the word "Total."

2) Staying in the same row as where you entered "Total," click in the cell under the frequency column. Now click on the auto sum button on the toolbar. $\Sigma \cdot$ You should see the following:

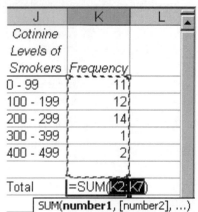

3) Press **Enter**, if the cells you want to add are the ones selected. If you want to include other cells than those automatically selected, you can select a range of cells before pressing **Enter.** You should now see the total number of data values in your data set, which should be 40.

4) At the top of the next column of your frequency distribution, type in the name "Relative Frequency." Again, click on another cell, and then re-click on the heading. Click on **Format,** and select **Cells.** Then under **Alignment,** make sure there is a check mark in front of "Wrap Text." Then click on **OK.**

5) Decide whether you want to have your relative frequencies displayed as decimals or percents. To change the formatting of the column, click on the letter at the top of the column to select the column, or select only the cells where your values will appear. Click on **Format,** and choose **Cells.** To match the chart in Table 2-3 of your book, in the **Number** tab of the dialog box, choose Percentage, and set the Decimal places to 0. Then click on **OK.**

6) In the cell immediately to the right of your data for the first class, enter the formula that will divide your frequency count for a class by the total number of data values. For example, if your first upper class limit is in cell J2, your frequency count for that class is in H2 and your total frequency count is in H8, you would type: =J2/$H$8, and press **Enter.** Notice that J2 (where your first frequency count can be found) is a relative address, while H8 (where the total of all frequencies can be found) is an absolute address, indicated by the $ signs. This will allow the numerator to be updated when you copy the formula, but will keep the total number of values (in this case, 40) fixed.

7) Copy this formula to fill in the remaining cells in your table. You should see a table similar to the following:

Cotinine Levels of Smokers	Frequency	Relative Frequency
0 - 99	11	28%
100 - 199	12	30%
200 - 299	14	35%
300 - 399	1	3%
400 - 499	2	5%
Total	40	

TO PRACTICE THESE SKILLS

To really learn how to use Excel well, you need to practice the skills covered in the previous section several times before you "own them."

1) Using the upper class limits of 99, 199, 299, 399, 499 and 599, create the frequency distributions for each of the sets of data **Smoker, ETS, NOETS.** Then create an additional column for each of these tables which show the relative frequencies as percents. Finally, using cut and paste, create a table in Excel similar to Table 2-7 in your book. **Note:** To paste a set of values that were initially generated by a formula, you should use the "Paste Special" option, and click on "Values." Otherwise you will be moving the formulas away from the cells that were used to create them, and you will not see the values you want pasted into the new column. Always make

sure you save your work, using a file name that will be indicative of the material contained in the Excel workbook. You will find you use many of the data sets more than once, and can utilize different worksheets within a file to separate the different work you do with the same data.

2) You can also practice your skills by using Excel to complete exercises 5 through 8 and 13 through 20 from Section 2-2 Basic Skills and Concepts in your textbook.

SECTION 2-3: PICTURES OF DATA

CREATING A HISTOGRAM

There are two situations you may find yourself in when asked to create a histogram: 1) You may only have the original data, in which case you can use the **Data Analysis, Histogram** feature in Excel; or 2) You may have an existing frequency distribution, in which case you can use the **Chart Wizard**.

CREATING A HISTOGRAM DIRECTLY FROM A DATA SET

1) Using the instructions from section 2-2 if necessary, repeat the steps to create a frequency distribution for the data on Cotinine Levels in Smokers. Remember, you will select **Tools, Data Analysis** and **Histogram.** In addition make sure that the box beside **Chart Output** is checked. If you saved your previous work, you can have the output placed underneath your original work.

2) Click on **OK.** You will see the information below in your worksheet.

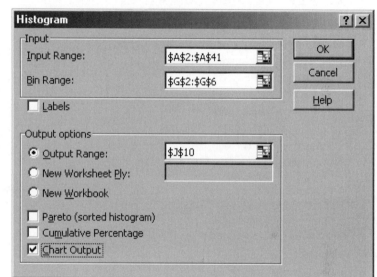

Bin	Frequency
99	11
199	12
299	14
399	1
499	2
More	0

Note:
Excel uses bin numbers that are the upper class limits, but they are typically printed in the center of the histogram bars. This is deceptive. Usually values in the middle of the bars are interpreted to be the class midpoint values. Make sure you modify your histogram as outlined below to rectify this situation.

MODIFYING THE HISTOGRAM

You will need to modify the histogram some to make it look the way you want it to. In particular, you will want to remove the extra column on the histogram entitled "More", change your values on the horizontal axis to either reflect class midpoints, or to show the classes, close the gap between the bars, re-name the horizontal axis, and give the graph an appropriate title. In addition, you will want to resize your graph. Instructions to complete the revisions follow.

Removing the extra column entitled "More"

You will want to remove the line that indicates "More" in both your frequency distribution and in your graph. To accomplish this, follow the steps below.

1) Highlight the two cells in the frequency distribution that you wish to remove.

2) Click on **Edit**, click on **Delete**, click in the bubble in front of **Shift Cells up**, then click on **OK**. Notice that when you did this, the extra column space entitled "More" also was deleted from your picture.

Removing the Gap Between Bars

1) To remove the gap between the bars on the Histogram, right click on one of the histogram bars.

2) Click on **Format Data Series** in the shortcut menu that is displayed. (You can also double click on one of the histogram bars to go directly to the Format Data Series dialog box.)

3) In the **Format Data Series** dialog box, click on the **Options** tab, and change the gap width value to 0. Click on **OK**.

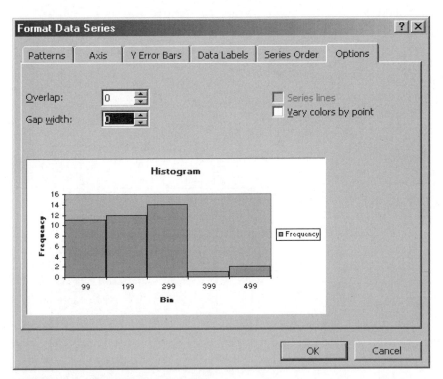

Changing the Values on the Horizontal Axis

As stated before, the values that are initially placed on the axis when creating a frequency distribution and histogram with the **Histogram** feature in the **Data Analysis** package, are the upper class limits, or bin values. Typically, you would expect to see either class midpoints on the horizontal axis, or a range of values indicating the various classes. To change the values along the horizontal axis, follow the steps below.

1) In your worksheet, type the values that you want to include on your horizontal axis in a column. You can type over the values that are initially printed out with your frequency distribution, using either classes, or class midpoints. On the worksheet used to create this manual, the classes themselves were

typed in to replace the bin values once the frequency distribution was created. These values appear in cells J2 to J6.

2) Click in the white area surrounding your histogram. When you hold your cursor there for a few seconds, you should see the tag "Chart Area" appear. When you click in this region, you will see that your chart is "selected," meaning that it has a box with corner and midpoint markers surrounding it.

3) With Chart Area selected, left click within the selected box. In the menu that appears, click on **Source Data,** and then click on the **Series** tab.

4) Click in the box entitled: "Category (X) Access Labels," and delete the text in that box. Then select the values in your worksheet that you want to put on the x axis. **You cannot merely type in range values. In this dialog box, you must select the appropriate cells directly from your worksheet.** Notice that when you select your cells, information about which sheet the values appear in is also included. Your dialog box should look something like the following:

5) Click on **OK**. Your histogram should now be displayed with the columns together, and should have more appropriate values along the horizontal axis.

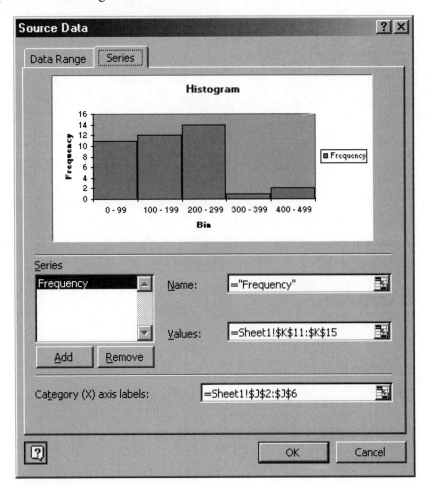

Changing the Graph Title and Axes Labels

The graph title that comes up on your histogram by default is "Histogram," and the x axis label is "Bins." Notice you also see a Legend box entitled "Frequency." You will want to change the names to be more indicative of what the graph represents, and you will want to delete the Legend. There are two ways that you can change the information initially listed on your histogram.

1) With the Chart Area selected, left click in this region, and then click on **Chart Options.**

2) In the "Chart Title" and "Category (X) Axis" boxes, type in more appropriate names for the graph and the values on the horizontal axis. Your dialog screen should look similar to the one shown below. Then click **OK.**

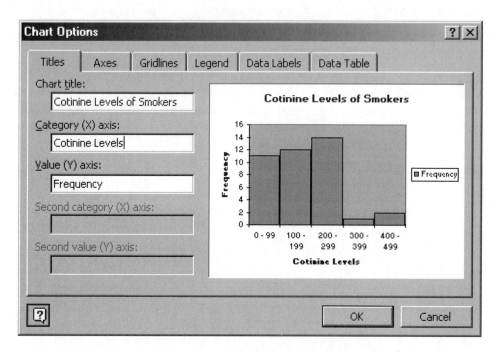

OR, alternatively:

1) Select the title or the axis name you want to change by clicking on it. Your title or axis name will have a "selection box" around it.

2) To change the name, simply begin typing the new name you wish to use. Notice the text is typed up at the top of the worksheet, and the title in the box is changed once you press **Enter**.

3) To delete a title, simply click on it to create the "handles," and then press **Delete.** If you delete a title, and later want to re-create it, select the Chart Area, right click, then click on **Chart Options** and click on the **Titles** tab.

Resizing a Region

1) Select the region you want to resize. Specifically, let's resize the entire "Chart Area."

2) Notice the black "handles" on the selection box.

   a) By clicking and dragging on the corner handles, you can resize the region in both directions.
   b) By clicking and dragging on the side handles, you can stretch or shrink the region horizontally.
   c) By clicking on the middle handles at the top or bottom, you can stretch or shrink the region vertically.

3) Move your cursor to the black box in the lower right hand corner. Your cursor should change to a double headed arrow. Left click, and holding the mouse down, drag this corner diagonally across your screen to resize the chart in both directions.

Realigning your Horizontal Axis Labels, and Changing the Font Size

The last changes we will make to the histogram will be to realign the horizontal axis labels, and to change the font size.

1) Move your cursor into the chart region near the horizontal axis until you see the tag "Category Axis" appear. Then right click, and click on **Format Axis.**

2) Click on the **Alignment** tab, and click on the red diamond shape near the word "Text." Holding your mouse down, drag the diamond to the positioning you want to use for your horizontal text. Then let the mouse key up.

3) Click on the **Font** tab, and make adjustments to your font size.

4) Explore the other possibilities if you would like, and then click on **OK**. Your histogram should now appear similar to the one below:

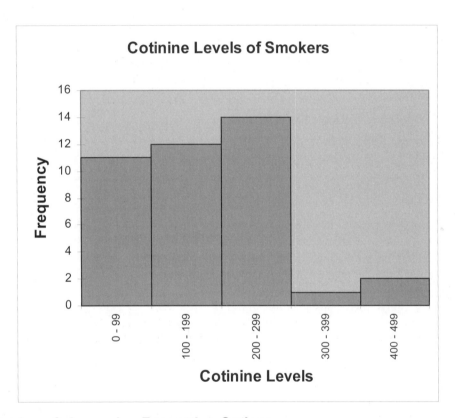

Selecting Regions & Accessing Formatting Options

1) Position your mouse over different parts of the white box containing the histogram. You will see "tags" come up telling you what the various regions are called. Regions include:

> Category Axis (Horizontal axis under the histogram where the "bin" values appear.)
> Chart Area
> Value Axis Title (Currently reads Frequency)
> Plot Area
> Chart Title (Initially reads Histogram)
> Category Axis Title (Initially reads Bins)

2) Click on a region and notice that "handles" appear around that region. This indicates that you have "selected" the region.

3) Right click while a region is selected to access the formatting menu. You have many options open to you in terms of what type of formatting changes you can make. We encourage you to "play" with the various options to create your own individualized picture.

CREATING A HISTOGRAM FROM A FREQUENCY DISTRIBUTION

If you already have a frequency distribution to start with, you can easily create a corresponding histogram by using the **Chart Wizard.** We will use this option to create the histogram for the relative frequency distribution that we developed in section 2-2. This table can also be found as Table 2-3 in your textbook.

1) In a new worksheet, type in the data from the relative frequency distribution of Cotinine Levels in Smokers. Before you type in the relative frequencies, format the column to show percentages with 0 decimal places. Click on the letter at the top of the column, then click on **Format**, click on **Cells**, click on the **Number** tab, click on **Percentages,** and change the number of decimal places to 0. Then click on **OK.**

2) You should have a table that looks like the following:

3) Once we have the table showing relative frequencies, we can employ the Chart Wizard to generate a relative frequency histogram from this data. There are a series of 4 linked dialog boxes that you need to address when using the Chart Wizard.

	A	B
1	Cotinine	Relative Frequency
2	0 - 99	28%
3	100 - 199	30%
4	200 - 299	35%
5	300 - 399	3%
6	400 - 499	5%

4) Click on **Insert** in the menu bar and click on **Chart**, or click on the **Chart Wizard** icon on the toolbar.

5) In Step 1 of 4, in the **Standard Types** menu, make sure that **Column** is highlighted. Then click on **Next** at the bottom of the screen. This will take you to the second dialog box.

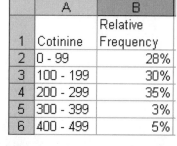

6) In the second dialog box (**Step 2 of 4 - Chart Source Data**) enter the range where your relative frequencies are listed by selecting these cells in the worksheet. Think of range as your output values, or what you want displayed on your vertical axis. Note that the name of your sheet comes up in the front of the range, and that the cell addresses are absolute addresses.

7) In this same dialog box, click on the **Series** tab, and click in the **Category (X) axis labels** box. Enter in the range where your upper class limits are listed by selecting the cells in your worksheet. **Note:** You **MUST** select the cells where your input values are located in your worksheet. You cannot enter the range of cells separated by a colon in this region. Your dialog box should look like the one shown here if you had your classes listed in cells A2 through A6 and the relative frequencies in cells B2 through B6.

8) Click on **Next.**

9) In Step 3 of 4 - **Chart Options**, type in an appropriate Title, and descriptions of your x and y axes if desired. Click on each tab at the top of the dialog box, and determine which components

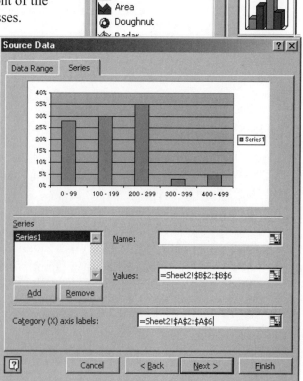

you wish to select. Your dialog box should look like the following:

10) Click on **Next.**

11) In Step 4 of 4 - **Chart Location**, determine whether you want your chart in a new worksheet (recommended option) or inserted in an existing worksheet. Then click on **Finish.**

12) You should now see a basic relative frequency histogram like the

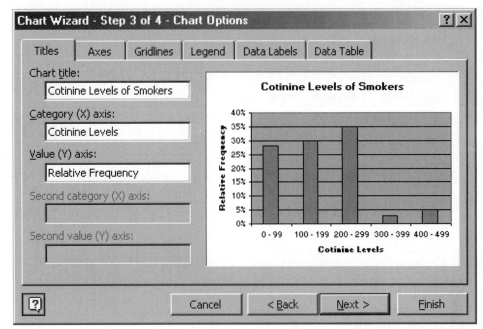

one shown below. Clearly, you will again want to modify the histogram by changing the gap width to 0, resizing the picture, realigning your horizontal axis labels, etc. See the previous instructions in this section to make appropriate modifications to your relative frequency histogram.

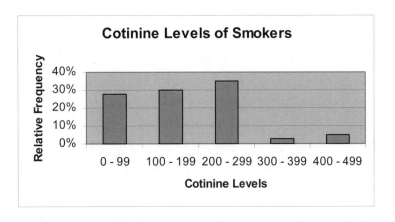

CREATING A FREQUENCY POLYGON

Once we have the frequency distribution for our data, we may choose to represent it graphically as a frequency polygon rather than a histogram. Since frequency polygons display points above the class midpoints, we first need to enter a new column for these values.

1) If you already have your frequency distribution for the Cotinine Levels of Smokers entered in a worksheet, you can simply add a column showing the class midpoints. This column can be entered directly next to the relative frequencies, or can be entered elsewhere on your worksheet. We have chosen to insert a column between the column containing the classes, and the column containing the relative

	A	B	C
1	Cotinine	Cotinine Midpoints	Relative Frequency
2	0 - 99	49.5	28%
3	100 - 199	149.5	30%
4	200 - 299	249.5	35%
5	300 - 399	349.5	3%
6	400 - 499	449.5	5%

frequencies. To do this, click on the letter at the top of your column for relative frequencies to select that entire column. Then click on **Insert,** and click on **Columns.** This will insert a column directly to the left of the one initially selected.

2) Type in the title "Cotinine Midpoints," and enter the midpoint values in the cells directly under this. Your midpoint values will be 49.5, 149.5, 249.5, 349.5 and 449.5. Your worksheet should be similar to the one shown on the previous page.

3) Click on **Insert** from the menu bar, and click on **Chart.**

4) Click on **Line** under **Chart Types,** and click on the first option in the second row of possible graph types. Your screen should look like the one shown. Then press **Enter**.

5) In the **Data Range** box, enter the range where the frequencies are located by selecting the appropriate cells in your worksheet.

6) Click on the **Series** tab at the top of the dialog box, and click in the **Category (X) axis labels** box. Then select the range of cells where your class midpoints are located. Then click on **Next.**

7) In Step 3 of 4 - **Chart Options**, type in an appropriate Title, and descriptions of your x and y axes if desired. Click on each tab at the top of the dialog box, and determine which components you wish to select. Then click on **Next.**

8) In Step 4 of 4 - **Chart Location**, determine whether you want your chart in a new worksheet (recommended option) or inserted in an existing worksheet. Then click on **Finish.** Your graph will look similar to the one below. Again, you will want to modify your chart by resizing it, and potentially making other changes, including changing the font sizes, to make it look more appealing.

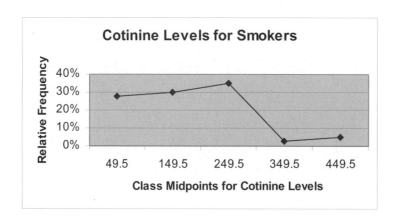

CREATING A PARETO CHART

We can use Excel to sort qualitative data in order of decreasing frequencies, and then call on the **Chart Wizard** to create a Pareto chart.

1) Enter the following table into a new worksheet in Excel. **Make sure you use adjacent columns!** You must have the data in contiguous columns in order to properly have the information sorted. Again, get in the habit of naming your worksheets. Double click on the worksheet tab, and type Pareto to indicate that this worksheet contains your work to create a Pareto chart.

Complaints Against Phone Carriers	Frequency
Rates and Services	4473
Marketing	1007
International Calling	766
Access Charges	614
Operator Services	534
Slamming	12478
Cramming	1214

2)   We first need to sort the data in order of decreasing frequency.   Click on any one cell containing a value in the Frequency column. Do **NOT** select the entire column!

3)   Click on **Data** in the menu bar, and then click on **Sort.**   Make sure that the Sort by box shows Frequency. Click inside the circle next to **Descending.** Your dialog box should look like the following:

4)   Click on **OK.** Your data should now be sorted from highest to lowest. You should see that the table labels were rearranged so that they stayed matched with the appropriate data value. Your table should look like the following:

5)   Click on **Insert**, then click on **Chart**, and click on **Column.** Follow through the 4 linked steps in the Chart Wizard. **Remember, when you enter a range, you should do so by selecting the appropriate cells in your worksheet**. Notice

	A	B
1	Complaints Against Phone Carriers	Frequency
2	Slamming	12478
3	Rates and Services	4473
4	Cramming	1214
5	Marketing	1007
6	International calling	766
7	Access Charges	614
8	Operator Services	534

that the name of your worksheet comes up in the front of the range, and that the cell addresses are absolute addresses.

6)   Enter your range where your frequencies are listed as the **Data range**.

7)   Click on the **Series** tab, and click inside the box near **Category (X) axis.** Then select the cells where your labels are located.

8)   Select appropriate titles and options under the **Chart Options** menu. When you are finished, your chart should look like the one below. Please make sure you follow procedures to refine your original picture!

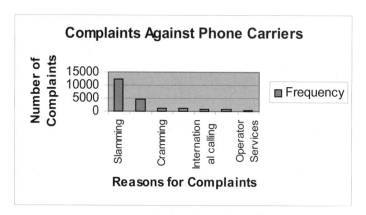

Modifying Your Pareto Chart

Once you have your basic picture, you should make further modifications to "professionalize" your chart. You should resize the chart, change the font size on the horizontal axis, and delete the "Series 1" legend box on the right hand side. You should also close the gap between the columns. Review various ways to modify the chart by re-reading material in this manual starting on page 22. A final picture of an appropriate Pareto Chart might appear as the one below.

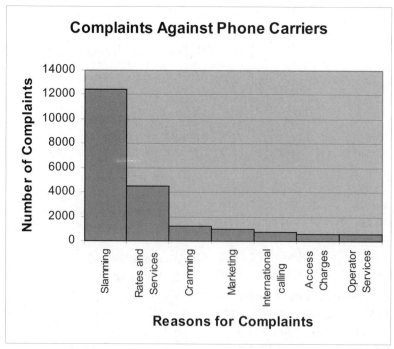

CREATING A PIE CHART

We may decide that we want to graphically show qualitative data on a pie chart, rather than as a Pareto chart. Let's work again with the information on Phone Company Complaints. The original data is listed below.

Complaints Against Phone Carriers	Frequency
Rates and Services	4473
Marketing	1007
International Calling	766
Access Charges	614
Operator Services	534
Slamming	12478
Cramming	1214

1) Enter this information into two adjacent columns in a new worksheet, or copy it into a new worksheet if you have already entered it for the Pareto chart. **Do not leave a column in between the sources and frequencies.**

2) Highlight the cells with the sources and frequencies.

3) Click on **Insert,** and then click on **Chart.** This will start you through a series of 4 linked dialog boxes.

4) In the **Chart Type** box (Step 1 of 4), click on **Pie**, and then select the type of pie chart you want in the **Chart sub-type** menu box. Then click on **Next** at the bottom of the screen.

5) The second dialog box is entitled **Chart Source Data**. Notice that your data range is already entered. This is due to the fact that in step 2 you highlighted the cells with the information in it before you began working through the Chart Wizard. If you had not selected the data in step 2, you would need to follow steps 6 through 8 under Creating a Pareto Chart. Click on **Next**

6) In Step 3 of 4, you can enter your **Chart Options**.

7) Click on the **Legend** tab, and indicate where you want the legend box to appear in relation to your pie chart.

8) Click on the **Data Labels** tab, and select what type of labels you want to use for your pie chart. Try clicking in front of each to see how they will appear on the graph. Click on **Next**.

9) In Step 4 of 4, you can enter where you want your **Chart Location**.

   - Placing your chart in a new sheet is recommended. If you choose this option, enter in a descriptive name for the sheet, such as "Pie Chart."
   - If you want your chart in an existing sheet, enter the sheet name or number. Pressing the down arrow at the end of the entry box will show a drop down menu of the current sheets available in your workbook.

10) Click on **Finish**.

Modifying Your Initial Pie Chart

You will now see your initial pie chart. You should experiment with resizing and reformatting the various parts of your chart. It is recommended that you resize the pie itself so that it takes up more of the Chart Area.

1) Move your cursor close to the circle until you see the tag **Plot Area** appear. Click once you see this tag appear, and you will see a rectangle with handles surround your circle. You can now resize the circle within the **Chart Area**.

2) Move your cursor over the labels until you see the tag **Data Labels**. Click once you see this tag appear. You will see handles appear by the various labels. Right click, and in the menu box which appears, highlight and click on **Format Data Labels**. Experiment with the different options available.

3) Move your cursor over the legend until you see the tag **Legend**. Click once you see this tag appear. Right click, and then click on **Format Legend**. Experiment with the different options.

PRINTING A GRAPH

You can elect to print only the final graph that you create.

1) Select the graph you wish to print by positioning your cursor somewhere in the **Chart Area**, and clicking once.

2) Click on **File**, and in the drop down menu which appears, click on **Print Preview**.

3) You should now see a screen shot of what your graph will look like when you print it.

4) You can change the page margins by first clicking on **Margins,** and then positioning your cursor on the dotted page guide you want to move. Your cursor should change into a double-headed arrow bisected by a straight line segment. Hold your left click button down and drag your cursor to the position you want the margin to be. Then release the mouse. You should see your page margins change in the direction you moved.

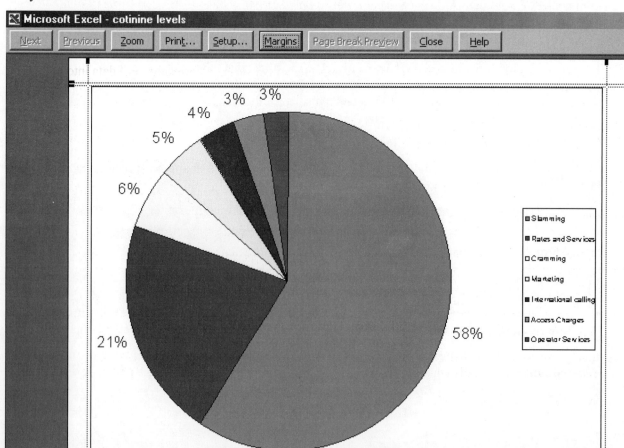

5) If you want to modify your graph, close the **Print Preview** window and make the changes you want to the graph.

6) Re-check your picture in the **Print Preview** window again. When your picture is as desired, press the **Print** key found at the top of the **Print Preview** window.

TO PRACTICE THESE SKILLS

You can apply the technology skills covered in this section by working through the following exercises. Make sure you save your work using a file name that is indicative of the material contained in your worksheets.

1) To practice constructing **histograms**, work on exercises 9 and 10 from Section 2-3 Basic Skills and Concepts in your textbook.

2) To practice constructing **frequency polygons**, work on exercises 11, 12, and 14 from Section 2-3 Basic Skills and Concepts in your textbook.

3) To practice creating **relative frequency histograms**, work on exercise 13 from Section 2-3 Basic Skills and Concepts in your textbook.

4) To practice creating a **Pareto Chart**, work on exercises 21 and 24 from Section 2-3 Basic Skills and Concepts in your textbook.

5) To practice creating a **pie chart**, work on exercises 22 and 23 from Section 2-3 Basic Skills and Concepts in your textbook.

SECTION 2-4 & 2-5: DESCRIPTIVE STATISTICS - MEASURES OF CENTER AND VARIATION

PRODUCING A SUMMARY TABLE OF STATISTICS USING DESCRIPTIVE STATISTICS

We will work again with the data from Data Set 6 in Appendix B (Measured Cotinine Levels in Three Groups). This data is also presented in Table 2-1 in your textbook. If you have already created a workbook for previous work with this data, open that file, and copy your original data to a clean worksheet. You can also load the data from the CD into a new file. If an electronic version of the data is not available to you, you should type the data from Appendix B, Data Set 6 into a new worksheet. Type each set of data into a separate column, one for Smoker, one column for the data on ETS, and one column for the data on NOETS. Again, if you are starting a new file, get in the habit of renaming the sheet that your original data is in "Original Data" by double clicking on the tab at the bottom of the worksheet, and typing in the name. Then copy your data to a new sheet to work with, so that you always have a version of your original data to refer back to if necessary.

1) Click on **Tools** in the menu bar, and then click on **Data Analysis.**

Note:

If **Data Analysis** does not show up as an option, you need to load this as an Add-In in Excel. Follow the directions in section 2-1 of this manual.

2) Click on **Descriptive Statistics**.

3) Suppose we want the statistics on the data for smokers. In the **Input Range** box, either type in the beginning and ending cells where your data is located, separating the 2 cells with a colon, or select these

cells in your worksheet. In the worksheet used to create this manual, this data could be found in column A, in cells A2 through A 41. Therefore, we could type **A2:A41** or we could select this range of cells.

4) Click in the circle before **Output Range**, and then click inside the white entry box. Then type in the cell where you want your statistics to begin appearing, or click in that cell in your worksheet. In the worksheet used to create this manual, the statistical output would begin in cell G2.

5) Click in the box before **Summary Statistics**, and then click on **OK**.

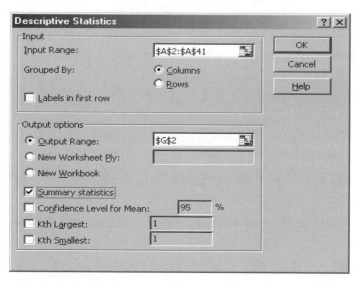

6) You will see your **Summary Statistics** displayed starting in the cell you indicated on your worksheet.

7) Resize your columns so that the full words can be seen. (You can do this by moving your cursor to the right hand side of the column name where you want to resize. Your cursor will turn into a double headed arrow with a straight line segment through it. When it does, double click, and your column will be automatically sized to fit the longest word in the column.)

8) Click on the title **Column 1** and type in "Statistics for Cotinine Levels in Smokers." Click on another cell, and then click back on your title, and format the cell to wrap the text. (Click on **Format,** choose **Cells,** then select **Alignment,** and click in the box next to **Wrap Text.**)

9) You may want to delete some of the standard choices from your list. Select the two cells that contain the information on Kurtosis, and press **Delete**. Do the same for Standard Error.

10) You now have empty rows in your table. Select all the information in the two columns of your table. Do not include the title in your selection box. Then click on the **Sort** icon from A to Z ![A/Z sort icon]. You will now see the information presented in alphabetical order, with the extra rows eliminated.

11) To remove the bottom bar, select the two cells containing the bottom border. Click on the down arrow by the frame icon, ![frame icon] and select the **No Border** icon in the displayed table ![border icon]. Your statistics should appear as shown in the table.

G	H
Statistics for Cotinine Levels in Smokers	
Count	40
Maximum	491
Mean	172.475
Median	170
Minimum	0
Mode	1
Range	491
Sample Variance	14279.84551
Skewness	0.587928591
Standard Deviation	119.4983076
Sum	6899

Interpreting the Output in the Descriptive Output Table

Below is a brief description of each of the measures included in Descriptive Statistics.

- **Mean:** The arithmetic average of the numbers in your data set.

- **Standard Error:** This is computed by using the formula $S / \sqrt{n}$ where S is the sample standard deviation and n is the number of observations.

- **Median:** This is the data value that splits the distribution in half. To determine the value of the median, the observations are first arranged in either ascending or descending order. If the number of observations is even, the median is found by taking the arithmetic average of the two middle values. If the number of observations is odd, then the median is the middle observation.

- **Mode:** This is the observation value associated with the highest frequency. **Caution:** Three situations are possible regarding the mode: 1) if all values occur only once in a distribution, Excel will return #N/A. 2) If a variable has only one mode, Excel will return that value. 3) If a variable has more than one mode, Excel will still return only one value. The value used will be the one associated with the modal value that occurs first in the data set. To check the accuracy of the mode, it would be wise to create a frequency distribution.

- **Standard Deviation:** This is computed using the formula: $S = \sqrt{\dfrac{\sum (X - \overline{X})^2}{n-1}}$

- **Sample Variance:** This is the standard deviation squared.

- **Kurtosis:** This number describes a distribution with respect to its flatness or peaked ness as compared to a normal distribution. A negative value characterizes a relatively flat distribution. A positive value characterizes a relatively peaked distribution.

- **Skewness:** This number characterizes the asymmetry of a distribution. Negative skew indicates that the longer tail extends in the direction of low values in the distribution. Positive skew indicates that the longer tail extends in the direction of the high values.

- **Range:** The minimum value is subtracted from the maximum value.

- **Minimum:** The lowest value occurring in the data set.

- **Maximum:** The highest value occurring in the data set.

- **Sum:** The sum of the values in the data set.

- **Count:** The number of values in the data set.

CREATING PARTICULAR SAMPLE STATISTICS USING THE FUNCTION WIZARD

If you just want to know particular values, without producing the entire table of Descriptive Statistics, you can use the **Function** wizard, and select just the options that you want to use.

1) Decide which values you want to compute. We will compute the Mean, Median, Mode and Midrange as shown in Table 2-8 of your book.

2) In a sheet different from where your original data is stored, copy the data on Smokers, ETS and NOETS found in Data set 6 in Appendix B. It is best to have this data in contiguous columns, with no blank columns in between.

3) In blank columns near your original data, type in the headings for your columns: Smokers, ETS and NOETS. In the column immediately preceding these columns, but beginning one cell down, type in the words Mean, Median, Mode, Midrange. Your worksheet should look something like the following.

E	F	G	H
	Smokers	ETS	NOETS
Mean			
Median			
Mode			
Midrange			

4) Select the cell next to **Mean**, and directly under the title **Smoker**. In your menu bar, click on **Insert**, and then click on **Function.** In the dialog box that appears, click on the down arrow at the end of the box titled "Select a Category," and select **Statistical**. You should now see a listing that shows all the statistical functions available in Excel. Notice that the functions are listed in alphabetical order. Scroll down the list until you find the function **Average**. Click on this function. Click on **OK**.

5) On the line with the input box by **Number 1**, click on the icon to collapse the box, and select the data in your worksheet for which you wish to compute the mean. In the worksheet used for this manual, that data was in cells A2:A41. Then click on the icon to re-expand your dialog box. Your box should look similar to the one shown. Click on **OK**. You should see the average for your data returned in the cell you had your cursor positioned in on your worksheet.

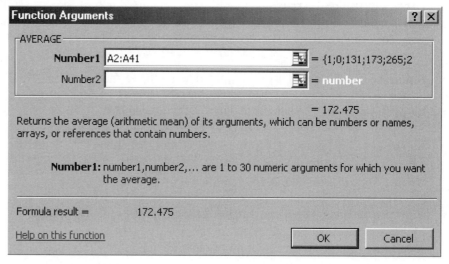

6) If your data for ETS and NOETS is in contiguous columns you can just copy the formula from your **Smokers Mean** cell to the cells representing **ETS Mean** and **NOETS Mean**. To do this, with your box containing the mean of smokers selected, click on **Edit,** and select **Copy**. Then select the adjacent two cells in your worksheet (where the information for ETS Mean and NOETS Mean should appear), and then click on **Edit, Paste.** To remove the "selection" box around your initial cell, press **Esc.**

7) If you have blank columns between the data for the other two groups, you can repeat the procedures from # 5, but each time select the appropriate cells for the average you are looking for.

8) Move your cursor to the cell for **Smokers Median**. Again, click on **Insert**, and select **Function**. This time, select the function **Median**, and then click **OK**. Again, in the **Number1** box, select, or type in the range of cells where the data for Smokers is found. Then click on **OK.** If your columns are contiguous, you can merely copy the formula from this cell to the other two cells you want to fill.

9) Move your cursor to the cell for **Smokers Mode**. Follow the same procedures as above, but select **Mode** from your **Function** dialog box. Notice that after you have completed entering the cells where the data for smokers is found, and have clicked on **OK,** only one of the modes is returned. Unfortunately Excel will only produce one mode, even if the data is multi-modal.

10) To make sure you have considered all modes, you can arrange the data in order, and visually look for other modes. To do this, Select the cells where your data for Smokers is located and select **Data, Sort.** Excel will return a **Sort Warning** box, as shown. Since you do not want the other columns to be affected, make sure that the bullet in front of "Continue with the current selection" and click on **Sort.**

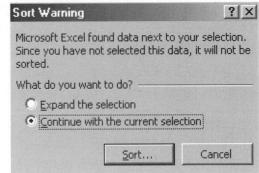

11) In the **Sort** Dialog box that appears, make sure that the bullet near **Ascending** is checked, and then click **OK.** Looking at the sorted data, you see that there are 2 values of 1. Scan through the column to see if any other data appears twice.

12) The next values we want are the midrange values. Excel does not have a direct way to compute the midrange. However, **if you order the data in ascending order**, as explained in steps 10 and 11above, you can easily create a formula that will return the midrange.

13) After sorting the data in each column, position your cursor in the cell where the value for **Smokers Midrange** would appear. Type in a formula similar to the following (your formula may differ depending on what cells your data for smokers is in): **= (A41-A2)/2** Remember, the = sign tells Excel that you are entering a formula. The parentheses are necessary in order to preserve the order of operations. Then press **Enter**.

14) Again, as long as your data is in contiguous columns, you can copy the formula in your **Smokers Midrange** cell to the other two cells. Otherwise, you can repeat the procedures for the other two values.

15) Your table should now look something like the one shown. You may have more or less decimal places. To create the same number of decimal places as shown in Table 2-8 of your book, select the cells that contain values, then click on **Format, Cells,** and choose **Number.** Change the number of decimal places to the number you want to use, and then click on **OK.**

E	F	G	H
	Smokers	ETS	NOETS
Mean	172.475	60.575	16.35
Median	170	1.5	0
Mode	1	1	0
Midrange	245.5	275.5	154.5

16) If you want to include a line for the **sample standard deviation** of your data, you would access the function **STDEV**, and again, select the cells containing the data for which you wanted to compute the sample standard deviation. Likewise, if you wanted the **sample variance**, you would access the function **VAR**, and select the cells containing the data for which you wanted to compute the sample variance. **NOTE:** Excel also allows you to compute the standard deviation and variance of a population, by selecting **STDEVP** and **VARP.**

COMPUTING THE MEAN FROM A FREQUENCY DISTRIBUTION

We can use Excel to create the mean from a frequency distribution, such as the one in Table 2-9 in your book. You should type in the information given in the first 3 columns of the table in 3 contiguous columns in Excel. Make sure you use appropriate column headings in your first row. You should format your columns so that they are wide enough to show the entire column heading, and you may want to center the data within each column to make your table look neater. You can center the information in all columns by selecting the columns and then accessing your **Center** icon in your toolbar.

1) In the column where you will show the frequency times the class midpoint, (the 4th column in Table 2-9) you will need to enter a formula. In the row where your first frequency and class midpoint are listed, type in the formula: = (cell reference where frequency is listed) * (cell reference where class midpoint is

listed). In the worksheet created for this problem, we typed in the following formula: =B2*C2. Then press **Enter.**

2) Position your cursor back in the cell where the product of the frequency and class midpoint appears. Then use the fill handle to copy the formula down the rest of the column.

3) For the mean, you want to divide the sum of the products of the frequency and the class midpoints by the sum of the frequencies. You will need to create the sums that you want to use by following the steps below.

4) Position your cursor in the cell directly under the last frequency, and select the summation key Σ ▾ in your toolbar. You want to add the values in the frequency column. This column should be automatically selected when you press the summation key, but if it is not, select the range of cells you want to sum up. Then press **Enter**.

5) Position your cursor in the cell directly under your last product of (frequency * class midpoint), and select the summation key from your toolbar Σ ▾. You want to add the values of the products in this column. Again, the column should be automatically selected when you press the summation key, but if it is not, select the range of cells you want. Then press **Enter.**

6) To find the mean, you want to divide the sum from your column of products by the sum of the frequencies. In the worksheet we created, we would represent this by the formula: = D7/B7. Notice that we entered this formula in cell g7, to create a result of 177.0.

7) Your worksheet should look similar to the following:

	A	B	C	D	E	F	G
1	Cotinine	Frequency	Class Midpoint	Freq * Midpoint			
2	0 -99	11	49.5	544.5			
3	100 - 199	12	149.5	1794			
4	200 - 299	14	249.5	3493			
5	300 - 399	1	349.5	349.5			
6	400 - 499	2	449.5	899			
7	Totals	40		7080		x bar	177.0

8) If you want to include more decimal places, you can select all the cells where you want more decimal places to appear, and select **Format,** then select **Cells, Number,** and set the number of decimal places to the number you wish to use. Then press **OK**.

COMPUTING THE STANDARD DEVIATION FROM A FREQUENCY DISTRIBUTION

Let's use the frequency distribution given in your book for Cotinine levels. As with finding the mean, you need to create a column that represents the (frequency * the class midpoint). You also need to create a column for the (frequency * square of the class midpoint).

1) Use the worksheet you set up to compute the mean of the frequency distribution if you have it saved, or create the worksheet from above, under the section "Computing the Mean from a Frequency Distribution." In the column directly after the column where you show the (frequency * class midpoint), create another column using a formula that shows the (frequency * square of the class midpoint). For the worksheet we used, our formula for the first row of data was: =B2 * C2^2 **NOTE:** To square a value, you use the carot (^) to indicate that the next value typed is the exponent.

2) As you did to compute the mean, use the summation key to sum up the values in that column.

3) Now we want to use the formula: $s = \sqrt{\dfrac{n[\sum(f \cdot x^2)] - [\sum(f \cdot x)]^2}{n(n-1)}}$. Think about what these values represent. The value n is the number of values included in the computation, so for this case, it will be the sum of the frequencies. We already have computed in the table the sum of the frequency times the square of the midpoint. We also have the value of the sum of the frequency times the midpoint. We need to create a formula that references the cells where these values are found. For the worksheet shown below, the formula we would enter to compute the value we want to find is: ==SQRT(((B7*E7)-D7^2)/(B7*(B7-1))). Make sure you think about where you need to put parentheses in order to maintain the appropriate order of operations. You need to make sure that you take the square root of the entire expression. Then you want to make sure you group the terms that represent the numerator. Finally, you need to group the factors that comprise the denominator. Look carefully how the parentheses shown group the various components together. This is a difficult expression to enter into Excel, because the grouping is essential in order to arrive at the appropriate answer. Your worksheet should look like the one shown below:

	A	B	C	D	E	F	G
1	Cotinine	Frequency	Class Midpoint	Freq * Midpoint	Freq * square of midpoint		
2	0 -99	11	49.5	544.5	26952.75		
3	100 - 199	12	149.5	1794	268203		
4	200 - 299	14	249.5	3493	871503.5		
5	300 - 399	1	349.5	349.5	122150.25		
6	400 - 499	2	449.5	899	404100.5		
7	Totals	40		7080	1692910	x bar	177.0
8							
9							
10					Standard deviation	106.1868	

TO PRACTICE THESE SKILLS

You can apply the skills learned in this section by working on the "Skills and Concepts" exercises found after section 2-4 and 2-5 in your textbook. **Notice that the data for the problems in Section 2-4 mirrors the data that is used again in the problems in Section 2-5.**

1) **To practice finding Measures of Center and Measures of Variation from data sets:** Work on the exercises 1 through 16 in both Sections 2-4 and 2-5 Basic Skills and Concepts in your textbook. For exercises 1 through 12, you will need to type the data into Excel. For exercises 13 through 16, you can load the data from the CD that comes with your book. As always, save your work with a file name that is indicative of the problem that you were working on.

2) **To practice finding the mean and standard deviation from a frequency distribution:** Work on exercises 17 through 20 in Sections 2-4 and 2-5 Basic Skills and Concepts in your textbook.

SECTION 2-6: MEASURES OF POSITION

Z-SCORES

When looking at a set of data, it is often useful to know how far a particular score falls from its mean. We can measure the position of a particular value with respect to the mean using z-scores. We know that if a value is more than 2 standard deviations away from the mean of the data set, it can be considered "unusual." Remember that whenever a value is below the mean, the corresponding z-score will be negative.

We will again work with the data from Data Set 6 in Appendix B (Measured Cotinine Levels in Three Groups). This data is also presented in Table 2-1 in your textbook.

- If you have already created a workbook for previous work with this data, open that file, and copy your original data for cotinine levels of smokers to a clean worksheet. (Remember, we recommend having one of your worksheets reserved just for the original data. Any time you want to use this data, we recommend that you copy it to another worksheet. That way you always have a copy of the original data to go back to if necessary.)
- You can also load the data from the CD into a new file.
- If an electronic version of the data is not available to you, you should type the data from Appendix B, Data Set 6 into a new worksheet. We will work only with the data for Smokers, so you can type that data into a column.

Again, if you are starting a new file, get in the habit of renaming the sheet that your original data is in "Original Data" by double clicking on the tab at the bottom of the worksheet, and typing in the name. Then copy your data to a new sheet to work with, so that you always have a version of your original data to refer back to if necessary.

We will create a column of z scores for the data on Smokers.

1) Create a worksheet that shows the data for smokers in column A. In order to create the z scores, we will need to know the mean and standard deviation for this data. In a column not contiguous to column A, use the function wizard to find the mean and standard deviation of this sample data. (You found these values back in sections 2-4 and 2-5, so refer back to those instructions if necessary.) In our worksheet, we created these values in cells D1 and D2.

2) If your original data is in column A, position your cursor in cell B1, and type "Standard Score."

3) Position your cursor in the cell directly beneath this heading. In our worksheet that is cell B2. From the **Function** menu (accessed either through **Insert, Function,** or by pressing the function icon), click on **Statistical** and **Standardized.**

4) In the dialog box, type in **A2** or the address where your first value is found. In the box for the **Mean,** type in the **absolute address** for the cell where your mean is found. In the worksheet we created, our mean was in cell D1, so we type in: $D$1. Notice that an absolute address, which will remain constant for all computations, whereas the x values will be updated when you use

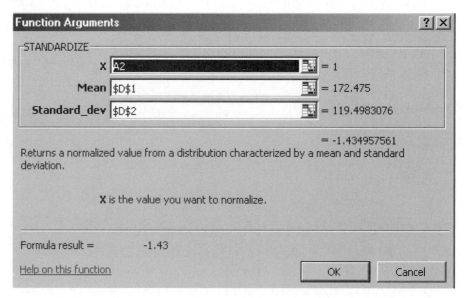

the fill command. In the box for the **Standard_dev**, type in the **absolute address** for the cell where your standard deviation is found. In the worksheet we created, our standard deviation is in cell D2, so we type in: $D$2. Your dialog box should look like the one shown.

5) Click on **OK**. You will now see the Standardized score for the first number in your data list in cell B2.

6) Since z-scores are normally reported to only two decimal places, you should format this column to show only two decimal places. Click on the letter at the top of your column for z-scores to select this whole column. Then click on **Format**, **Cells**, and **Number**, and then indicate 2 in the box by Decimal Places. Click on **OK**. You should now see the value for the z scores rounded to 2 decimal places. In our example, the first value in the table is 1, and we see a z score of -1.43. This indicates that the value of 1 is 1.43 standard deviations below the mean. Make sure you agree with this. The mean for our example is 172.475. The standard deviation is 119.498. If we subtract the mean from our value (1), and then divide by the standard deviation, we find that we do get a number which rounds to -1.43.

7) Use the fill handle to copy the formula down for the rest of the values in your data set. Notice that your values have z-scores ranging from –1.44 (indicating that 0 is 1.44 standard deviations below the mean) to 2.67 (indicating that 491 is 2.67 standard deviations above the mean).

Measures of Position

We can use Excel to find the three Quartiles, ten Deciles or 99 Percentiles for a data set. There are two functions within Excel that allow us to do this quickly: **Quartiles** and **Percentile**. There is no function for Deciles, but by recognizing that Deciles are the 10th, 20th, 30th, etc. percentiles, we can easily use the Percentile function to create the Decile values.

FINDING THE VALUES OF THE QUARTILES

1) Using the data on Cotinine Levels for Smokers, copy the data to column A of a new worksheet.

2) Suppose we want to find the first, second and third quartiles for the data. In cell C1, type in "Quartile." In cells C2 through C4, type in 1, 2, and 3.

3) Move your cursor to cell D2 and click on the **Function** icon on your menu bar, or click on **Insert, Function.**

4) Under **Function Category**, click on **Statistical**. Under **Function name**, click on **Quartile.**

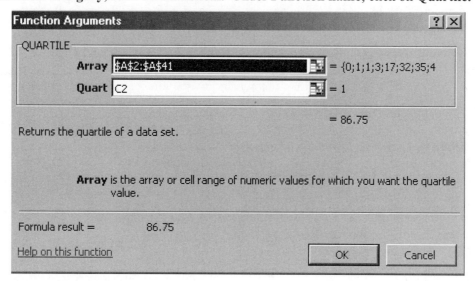

5) In the dialog box, in the Array box, **you must enter your range of cells using absolute addresses**. If you just select the cells, or just type in the range with a colon, the proper set of values will not be used when you copy the formula for the 2nd and 3rd quartiles! For our worksheet, the data appears in cells A2 through A41. In the **Quart** box, type in the cell where your first quartile appears. In our worksheet, this value of 1 appears in cell C2. Then click on **OK**.

6) You should see that the first quartile is the value 86.75. Roughly speaking, this means that if you sorted the original data values, about 25% of the sorted values in your table would be less than or equal to 86.75. We can say that at least 25% of the sorted values will be less than or equal to 86.75 and at least 75% of the sorted values will be greater than or equal to 86.75.

7) Use the fill handle to copy the formula down into the next two cells. You should see the values below:

C	D
Quartile	Value
1	86.75
2	170
3	250.75

8) To see that these values make sense in terms of your data, select column A by positioning your cursor on the A at the top of the column, and clicking once. Your entire column should now be selected. Then click on the **Sort** icon which shows from A to Z in your menu bar. This means that your data will be sorted from smallest to largest value.

Note:

Notice that there are 10 values which are less than or equal to 86.75. Since 10/40 represents 25%, we can see that **at least** 25% of the data values are less than or equal to 86.75. If we counted the values that were less than or equal to 170, we would find that 20 out of the 40 values fall into this category. Doing the division, we find that 20/40 = 50 %. We can say that **at least** 50% of the values are less than or equal to 170.

There are 30 values which are less than 250.75. Since 30/40 is 75%, we can see that **at least** 75% of the data values are less than or equal to 250.75.

FINDING THE VALUES FOR PERCENTILES

Let's now calculate the 10th, 20th, 30th,....,90th percentiles. These values will correspond to the 1st, 2nd, 3rd,...., 9th deciles.

1) Using our previous worksheet where we computed the quartiles, position your cursor in cell F1 and type in "Percentile." Starting in cell F2, enter the values 0.1, 0.2, 0.3, 0.4,....., 0.9. (Notice that Excel requires that you show the decimal form of the percentile that you want to find. 0.1 refers to the 10th percentile, since 0.1 is the decimal form of 10%.)

2) Move to cell G2, and click on the **Function** icon on the main toolbar. Click on **Percentile** from the **Statistical** menu. In the dialog box, indicate that the **Array** is stored in cells A2 to A41, again **using absolute addresses!** If you do not use the absolute addresses, when you copy

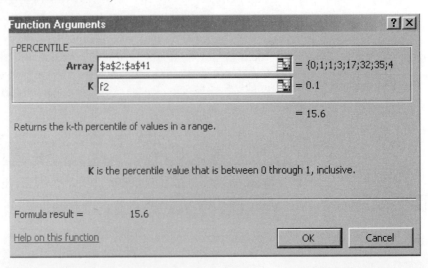

your formula, you array values will change. Indicate that the k value (for the kth percentile) is stored in cell F2. Click on **OK.**

3) You should now see the value 15.6 in cell G2. Use the fill handle to copy the formula down the rest of the column. You should see the following table:

F	G
Percentile	
0.1	15.6
0.2	47.2
0.3	109.3
0.4	130.6
0.5	170
0.6	208.8
0.7	237.3
0.8	265.2
0.9	289.1

4) Remember that the values can be used to talk about what percent of values in the data set are less than or equal to these values. For example, at least 60% of the values in the table should be less than or equal to 208.8. If you order your data for Cotinine level of Smokers, you can see that there are 24 values less than 208.8. If you divided 24/40, you would see that there are 60% of the values in the table which are less than or equal to 208.8.

5) If you had a different percentile, you would just enter the appropriate decimal value for k. For example, if you wanted the 35th percentile, you would use a k value of .35.

FINDING THE PERCENTILE FOR A PARTICULAR VALUE

Sometimes you want to know the percentile that corresponds to a particular value in a data set. You can use features of Excel to help you quickly determine this, particularly if your data set is large. For a small data set, it is probably just as easy to follow the procedures outlined in your book without calling on Excel. Let's consider finding the percentile for the cotinine level of 112 in Smokers.

1) The first thing you want to do is sort the data you are working with. If we are using the cotinine levels of smokers, we would want to sort the data in that column. Copy the data for cotinine levels of smokers into a new worksheet. Then click on the letter at the top of your column to select the entire column.

Then press the **Sort Ascending** key in your toolbar ⏬, or select **Data, Sort,** and then make sure that the bullet in front of Ascending is checked. Your data should then be sorted from lowest to highest value.

2) Position your cursor in a cell in a nearby column, and press **Insert, Function,** or click on the function icon in your toolbar. You want to count the number of values less than 112 in this case, so select **Count,** and click **OK**.

3) In the **Value1** box, enter the range of cells which contain numbers less than 112 in your sorted column, or select those cells with your cursor. Then click on **OK**. You should see the value 12 returned in your cell. This tells you that there are 12 values less than 112 in your sorted list. **It is imperative that you work with a sorted list!**

4) Since there are 40 values in the data set, you want to divide the number of values less than 112 by 40, and then multiply the result by 100. You can set up a formula in Excel to accomplish this. You would enter the formula as follows: = (cell where count is found)/40*100. In the worksheet we used, we used the formula: =C2/40*100, and received the answer of 30. This means that 112 is the 30th percentile.

5) If you were going to compute the percentile for a number of values, you could set up a worksheet as shown below. Though you have to change the cells within the **Count** function each time, since the number of values you want to count changes with each value for which you are finding the percentile, once you set up the formula for your last column in the first row, you can copy the formula to the other rows. The table below shows the percentiles for the values 112, 210 and 290.

B	C	D
Value	# of values < given value	Percentile
112	12	30
210	24	60
290	36	90

TO PRACTICE THESE SKILLS

1) **To practice finding z-scores:** You can work on the exercises 11 and 12 from Section 2-6 Basic Skills and Concepts in your textbook.

2) **To practice finding percentiles and quartiles:** You can work on exercises 25 through 36 from Section 2-6 Basic Skills and Concepts in your textbook.

SECTION 2-7: EXPLORATORY DATA ANALYSIS

In order to work on the material in this section, you will need to load the **DDXL** Add-In that is supplied with your book.

LOADING DDXL

1) Put the CD that comes with your book into your CD drive on your computer.

2) Press **Start**, and then select **Run** from the toolbar at the bottom of your Windows screen.

3) In the Run Dialog box, press **Browse**, and double click on the drive containing your CD. This drive should now show the name "Triola" indicating that the disk in the drive is the disk that accompanies your textbook.

4) Double click on the file folder that says **Software.**

5) One of the options in this folder is the **DDXL** program. Double clicking on this option will show 2 further options. Double click on the option that says "Install DDXL."

6) You should be taken back to your Run Dialog box, and should now see something similar to the following in the box: "E:\Software\DDXL\Install DDXL.exe." Press **OK**. You will be taken through the Install Wizard for the program. Follow the instructions on the screen. **Make sure you pay attention to where the program is being installed!** You will need to know this to add the program into your Excel program. Typically the install process will add the program to your hard drive in your Program Files Folder.

7) Open Excel, and from the main menu bar, select **Tools, Add-Ins.** Then click on **Browse.**

8) Click on the pull down arrow at the end of the "Look In" box. Select the location where the DDXL program was installed. Again, typically you will select your C drive, and then select the Program Files Folder. Once there, you should see a folder called DDXL. Clicking on this opens up a screen which

should show "DDXL Add-In." Select this option by either double clicking on it, or by clicking on it and then pressing **OK.**

9) You will be taken back to your Excel Add-In Selection Box, and you should see "DDXL Add-In" listed with a check in the box preceding the name. Click on **OK.**

10) You should now see DDXL listed in the main menu bar.

BOXPLOTS

Excel is not designed to generate boxplots. You can use the **DDXL** Add-In that is supplied with your book to generate this type of graph.

1) Open a worksheet where you have the data on Cotinine Levels for Smokers entered in column A. Make note of the range where your actual values are stored. If you entered the name Cotinine levels in cell A1, and the data directly below this, your values will be contained in cells A2:A41.

2) Click on the **DDXL** command on the main menu bar.

3) Select **Charts and Plots**. Under the **Function Type**, select the option **Boxplot**.

4) Click on the **pencil** icon at the bottom of the screen on the left hand side. Type in the cells where your data is stored in your Excel worksheet. In this case, you should type in A2:A41. Click on **OK** in the bottom right hand side of the screen. You will be taken to the **DDXL** screen which should appear as the one displayed below.

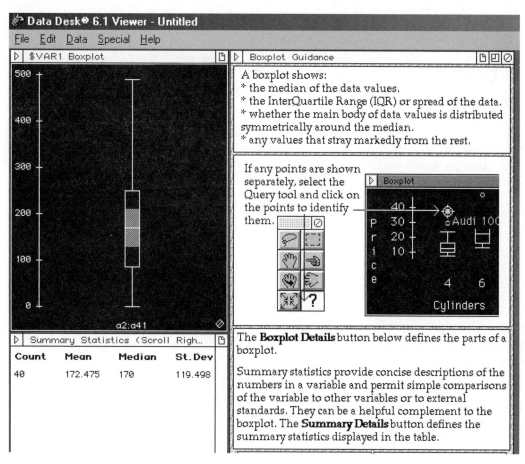

5) Notice that the boxplot is in the upper left hand corner, and that the Summary Statistics box can be found directly below that.

6) Click on the triangle in the upper left corner of the **Boxplot** screen, and select **Plot Scale**. Notice that you can change the settings for the Y axis as shown in the **Scale Plot** window. Make changes if you so desire, and then click on **OK**.

8) Click and hold on the diamond shape in the lower right hand corner of the **Boxplot** screen, and drag this corner out to create a larger graph if you would like.

9) Click anywhere in the **Summary Statistics** window to activate that screen. Again, click and hold on the diamond in the lower right hand corner of this box, and drag to the right to expand the amount of the box that can be seen. You want to be able to see all the scores shown in the chart on the next page. Notice that different programs can produce slightly different values for the different percentiles. We found the 3rd quartile (or 75th percentile) in Excel to be 250.75, while DDXL shows it to be 251.5. Though you may see some inconsistency in the exact values returned between programs, any value you get should be in the same general ballpark!

Summary Statistics (Scroll Right)										
Count	Mean	Median	St.Dev.	Variance	Range	Min	Max	IQR	25th%	75th%
40	172.475	170	119.498	14279.846	491	0	491	165	86.5	251.5

TO PRACTICE THESE SKILLS

You can apply the technology skills covered in this section by working through the exercises 1 through 12 from Section 2-7 Basic Skills and Concepts of your textbook. Remember that you may have already loaded some data from the CD into an Excel workbook for work from a previous section. You can open this file, and create a new worksheet within the file for any additional work you do with this particular data set.

CHAPTER 3: PROBABILITY

SECTION 3-1: OVERVIEW

This chapter in your textbook covers the basic definitions and concepts of probability. While many of those concepts are straightforward and can be done without the use of technology there are some features of Excel that can be utilized while working through the material found in this chapter. The following list contains an overview of the topics and functions that will be introduced within this chapter.

PIVOT TABLE
This feature is used to generate a worksheet table that summarizes data from a data list. This allows you to obtain category counts.

RANDBETWEEN
This function creates columns of random numbers that fall between the numbers you specify. A new random number is returned every time the worksheet is calculated. The function appears in the following format: **RANDBETWEEN (bottom, top)** where bottom is the smallest integer RANDBETWEEN will return and top is the largest integer RANDBETWEEN will return.

FACT
This function returns the factorial of a number. The factorial of a number is equal to $1 \cdot 2 \cdot 3 \cdot \ldots \cdot$ number. **FACT(number)** where number refers to the nonnegative number you want the factorial of. If number is not an integer, it is truncated.

PERMUT
This function returns the number of permutations for a given number of objects that can be selected from a larger group of objects. A permutation is any set or subset of objects or events where internal order is significant.
PERMUT(number, number_chosen) where number is an integer that describes the number of objects and number_chosen is an integer that describes the number of objects in each permutation.

COMBIN
This function returns the number of combinations for a given number of items. Use COMBIN to determine the total possible number of groups for a given number of items.
COMBIN (number, number_chosen) where number is the number of items and number_chosen is the number of items in each combination.

SECTION 3-2: PIVOT TABLES

In Excel it is possible to generate a table, called a **pivot table,** which can be used to summarize both quantitative and qualitative variables contained within a database. A **pivot table** provides us with a mechanism for creating subgroups (or samples), and gives us the ability to find sums, counts, averages, standard deviation and variance of both a sample and population.

CREATING A PIVOT TABLE:

We will create a pivot table using the data from Data Set 22 in Appendix B. This data can also be found on the CD-ROM data disk that accompanies your textbook. Begin by opening Excel. Open the data file "CARS."

Excel provides a **PivotTable Wizard** similar to the ChartWizard you have used to generate tables and graphs.

To create a Pivot Table:

1) On the menu bar click on **Data**, highlight **Pivot Table and Pivot Chart Report** and click.

The Pivot Table and PivotChart Wizard – Step 1 of 3 dialog box will appear. Make sure that both **Microsoft Excel list or database** and **PivotTable** are selected. Then click on **Next**.

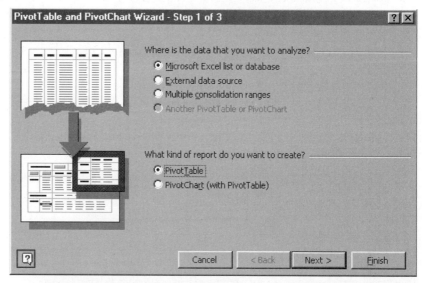

2) Indicate the worksheet range that contains the data you want to use. This may already be indicated when the dialog box opens. To select the data that you want to use drag the cursor across from cell A1 to cell I21. In the **Range window** you should see Sheet1!$A$1:$I$21. Click on **Next**.

3) The third dialog box of the PivotTable and PivotChart Wizard will ask if you want the Pivot Table in a new worksheet or in the existing worksheet. Once you have made your choice click on **Finish**.

4) Depending on where you chose to place your Pivot Table you will see the following on your current worksheet, or in a separate worksheet.

-   The small Pivot Table box displays a graphical layout of an empty pivot box as well as field buttons that correspond to the columns in your Excel worksheet.

-   You can specify the layout of the table by dragging fields into any of the four areas shown.

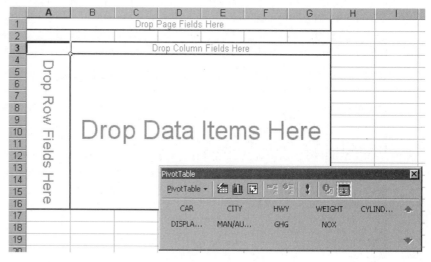

- You can drag as may field buttons as you like. If you make a mistake or wish to change the field button you moved, simply drag the field button back to the Pivot Table box. You can rearrange the Pivot Table as necessary.

5) To help you create your first Pivot Table

   a) Drag MAN/AUT to **Drop Page Fields Here**
   b) Drag CITY to **Drop Column Fields Here**
   c) Drag HWY to **Drop Row Fields Here**
   d) Drag MAN/AUT to **Drop Data Fields Here**

The table you create will display the number of city and highway miles broken down by the type of transmission (manual or automatic).

Count of MAN/AUTO	CITY									
HWY	17	18	19	20	22	23	28	29	32	Grand Total
24	2									2
26	2									2
27			3							3
28		1								1
29				2						2
30			1		1	1				3
31						1				1
32						2				2
33					1					1
34								1		1
37							1		1	2
Grand Total	4	1	4	2	2	4	1	1	1	20

(MAN/AUTO: (All))

6) Click on the **down arrow** by MAN/AUTO (All) to see the data summary for only manual transmissions (M) or only automatic transmissions (A).

Note:
Once you have created a Pivot table you can refine it. Right click on any cell within the Pivot Table for a list of options. The Wizard option will take you back to the Pivot Table Wizard used to create your existing table. Double click on the **field button** within the Pivot Table to open the Pivot Table Field dialog box for options concerning fields. As always, we encourage you to explore and experiment with the different options available to you.

PROBABILITIES

The pivot table shown on the next page was created to display the number of highway miles and its relationship to the type of car transmission (automatic or manual). Using a pivot table allows you to determine probability information more easily than sorting through the information presented to you in the original Excel worksheet.

Count of MAN/AUTO	MAN/AUTO		
HWY	A	M	Grand Total
24	2		2
26	2		2
27	3		3
28		1	1
29	1	1	2
30	2	1	3
31	1		1
32	1	1	2
33		1	1
34	1		1
37	1	1	2
Grand Total	14	6	20

TO PRACTICE THESE SKILLS

Use the information presented in the following Excel worksheet to create a Pivot Table that will display the total number of credits broken down by Religion and Major for
   a)   male and female students combined
   b)   only female students
   c)   only male students

	A	B	C	D	E	F
1	SEX	AGE	MAJOR	CREDITS	GPA	RELIGION
2	M	22	Liberal Arts	19	2.5	Jewish
3	M	23	Computer Science	14	3.7	Protestant
4	F	19	Criminal Justice	17	3.8	Protestant
5	M	22	Mathematics	18	2.4	Protestant
6	F	21	English	13	2.5	Jewish
7	F	23	Liberal Arts	18	3	Catholic
8	F	22	Liberal Arts	17	3.2	Catholic
9	M	22	Liberal Arts	18	3.6	Protestant
10	M	22	Education	13	3.5	Catholic
11	F	21	English	17	2.7	Protestant
12	F	22	Criminal Justice	15	2.5	Catholic
13	M	23	Computer Science	15	3.9	Jewish
14	F	22	Computer Science	17	3.3	Jewish
15	M	21	Engineering	12	2.5	Protestant
16	F	22	Engineering	18	4	Protestant
17	F	21	Mathematics	16	3.6	Catholic
18	F	22	Liberal Arts	18	3.4	Jewish
19	M	19	English	17	2.9	Jewish
20	M	21	Criminal Justice	17	3	Catholic
21	F	20	Engineering	16	2.8	Catholic

SECTION 3-3: GENERATING RANDOM NUMBERS

Begin by making cell A1 your active cell.

1) To generate a random set of numbers in Excel, click on **Insert**, highlight **Function** and click. The following **Paste Function Dialog box** will open. We have already made use of Excel's built in Statistical functions in previous sections.

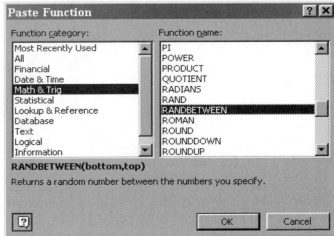

    a) To generate random numbers highlight **Math & Trig** as seen on the right.

    b) Scroll through the list of function names and highlight **RANDBETWEEN.**

    c) Click **OK.**

2) The dialog box, shown on the next page, should now be located in the upper left-hand corner of your Excel worksheet. Fill in the lowest and highest values between which the random number will fall. For example, if you wish to generate a list of possible values that can occur when you roll a single die then the bottom number would be 1 and the top value would be 6. Click **OK.**

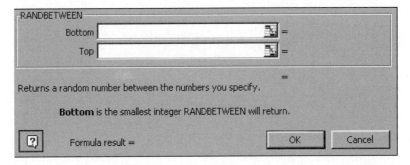

A random number between 1 and 6 should now appear in cell A1. To generate 25 such numbers copy (by dragging) this cell entry to cell A25. When you have completed this task you should have 25 entries in the first column, each between 1 and 6. A new random number is returned every time the worksheet is calculated.

SECTION 3-4: PROBABILITIES THROUGH SIMULATION

The goal of every statistical study is to collect data and to use that data to make a decision. Often collecting data or repeating a trial a large number of times can be impractical. With the use of technology we can often simulate an event.

Using the definition from the textbook: *"A simulation of a procedure is a process that behaves in the same ways as the procedure so that similar results are produced."*

The random number generator can be used to simulate a variety of statistical problems.

CREATING A SIMULATION

Let's consider the **Gender Selection example** presented in section 3-6 of your textbook. We can simulate 100 births.

1) Begin by opening a new worksheet in Excel. Make cell A1 your active cell.

2) Using the method outlined above simulate 100 births. Let 0 = male and 1 = female.

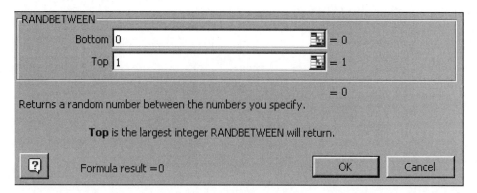

3) You can copy the information through to cell A100 or you can copy it through to cell A25. You can then copy the information into columns B, C and D. The advantage of this second method is that you can see the 100 entries in your simulation. You may notice that the entry in your first cell change. Don't worry about this. The cells will continue to change until we do our statistical analysis.

4) To determine the probability that the newborn if female, count the number of 1's in your data and divide by the total number of entries.

It might be interesting to repeat the simulation several times and compare your results.

Simulating Multiple Events

Consider a problem that requires more than one event to occur such as the probability of a specific sum when two dice are tossed as mentioned in the **Simulating Dice example** found in Section 3-6.

For the purpose of this simulation example we wish to find the P (sum of 5) when two dice are tossed 50 times. One possibility would be to toss a pair of dice 50 times and record the sums after each roll. Using technology to simulate this experiment we will produce similar results.

1) Begin in a new worksheet with cell A1 as the active cell. Type "First Die" in cell A1, type "Second Die" in cell B1 and type "Sum" in cell C1.

2) Begin in cell A2. Generate a *column* of 50 random values between 1 and 6.

3) Repeat the process beginning in cell B2. As before, you may notice that the cell entries in your first column change. This is normal. The cells will continue to change until we do our statistical analysis.

4) In cell C2 type =Sum (A2 + B2) and press **Enter**.

5) Copy this formula down through to cell C51. This should give you the sums of the toss of two dice. Once again you will notice that the entries in your first two columns have changed. This is normal. You

should be able to see rather easily that the sum of the first two column entries is reflected in the third column.

6) At this point it is possible to determine how many of our simulated tosses of the dice yield a sum of 5.

TO PRACTICE THESE SKILLS

You can practice the Excel skills learned in Sections 3-3 and 3-4 of this manual by working through the following problem.

1) Some role-playing games use dice that contain more sides than the traditional six sided dice most of us are familiar with. Assume we are playing such a game and that we are using a pair of ten sided dice which contain the numbers one through ten each die.
   a) Use the Random Number Generator to simulate rolling a pair of ten sided dice fifty times.
   b) Use the results to determine a list of possible sums from the fifty rolls of the dice.
   c) Find the probability of rolling a sum of 20.

2) Develop a simulation using Excel for Exercises 9 and 10 in the Basic Skills and Concepts for Section 3-6.

SECTION 3-5: FACTORIAL

In looking at the **Cotinine in Smokers** example found in section 3-7 of the textbook we found that we were required to multiply $3 \cdot 2 \cdot 1$. This product can be represented by 3! which is read as "three factorial." What appears to be an exclamation point after the 3 is really a **factorial symbol (!).** The factorial symbol indicates that we are to find the product of decreasing positive integers.

In Excel we can locate the **factorial function** using the same method we did for generating a random number.

1) Click on **Insert**, highlight **Function** and click. The **Paste Function Dialog box** will open.

2) Highlight **Math & Trig**

3) Scroll through the function names and highlight **FACT.**

4) Click **OK**

5) In the **FACT** dialog box enter that number you wish to expand by using factorials. **FACT(3)** equals $3 \cdot 2 \cdot 1 = 6$

6) Click **OK**

SECTION 3-6: PERMUTATIONS AND COMBINATIONS:

Problems involving permutations and combinations such as those found in section 3-7 of your textbook can be done fairly quickly and quite easily with Excel. A permutation is an ordering or arrangement of any set or subset of objects or events where order is significant. Permutations are different from combinations, for which the order is not significant.

The **PERMUT (permutations)** function can be found in the Function Dialog box in the **Statistical** function category.

The **COMBIN (combinations)** function can be found in the Function Dialog box in the **Math and Trig** function category.

Consider the **Television Programming example** found in Section 3-7 of your textbook. Use the **PERMUT function dialog** box:

Number – an integer that refers to the total number of objects - in this case 27 shows available.

Number_chosen - an integer that identifies the number of objects in each permutation. – in this case 4.

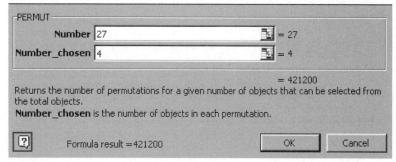

The result is 421,200 different possible arrangements of 4 shows selected from the 27 that are available.

Consider the **Elected Offices example** found in Section 3-7 of your textbook. Note that we use combinations for part (a) of this problem because order does not count and permutations for part (b) because order does count. Use the **COMBIN function dialog** box:

Number - the number of items – in this case 9 members.

Number_chosen - the number of items in each combination – in this case 3 person committee

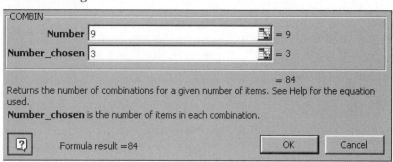

There are 84 different possible committees of 3 board members.

TO PRACTICE THESE SKILLS

You can practice the Excel skills learned in this section of this manual by working through the problems 3, 7, 17, and 21 from the Basic Skills and Concepts for Section 3-7.

CHAPTER 4: PROBABILITY DISTRIBUTIONS

SECTION 4-1: OVERVIEW

Excel has functions built into it that can be used to calculate the probabilities associated with several different probability distributions. Computing these probabilities by hand can be very time consuming. Although tables are available for some distributions, these are also limited in scope. Excel provides you with a tremendous amount of flexibility in creating these distributions quickly and efficiently. The following list contains an overview of the new functions that will be introduced within this chapter.

FILL SERIES
This feature enables us to quickly and efficiently enter a string of consecutive numbers in a column or row.

BINOMDIST
This function returns the individual term binomial distribution probability.

POISSON
This function returns the Poisson probability that a particular number of occurrences of an event will occur over some interval.

SECTION 4-2: RANDOM VARIABLES AND PROBABILITY DISTRIBUTIONS

We will consider the probability distribution for Probabilities of Girls given in Table 4-1 of your book. We will work with the values given, and create a probability histogram, as well as consider how we can use Excel to compute the mean and standard deviation of this probability distribution.

1) Open a new worksheet. Again, it is a good idea to get in the habit of entering the data in a worksheet entitled "Original Data." You can then copy the data to another worksheet, and work with the data there, ensuring that you always have ready access to the original data if needed.

2) Type "x" in cell A1 of a new worksheet, and "P(x)" in cell B1. Then enter the values given in Table 4-1 starting in cells A2 and B2 respectively.

3) Select this data, and copy it to another worksheet. Give your new worksheet an appropriate name that will remind you what is there. You might want to call the worksheet something like "prob dist." to indicate that you have the probability distribution in this sheet.

4) Click on the **Chart Icon**, or click on **Insert** in the menu bar, then click on **Chart.**

5) Click on **Column** under **Chart Type** and the first option under **Chart sub-type**. Then click on **Next.**

6) With your cursor positioned in the dialog box by **Data Range**, select the cells containing your probabilities. In the worksheet we set up, this would be cells B2 through B16. Notice that the box will show ='prob dist'!$B$2:$B$16 if you named your sheet "prob dist."

7) Make sure that the bubble in front of **Columns** is selected.

8) Click on the **Series** tab, and position your cursor in the dialog box by the word **Category (X) axis labels**. Select the cells containing the x values. In the worksheet we set up, this would be cells A2 through A16. Notice that the box will show ='prob dist'!$A$2:$A$16 if you named your sheet "prob dist."

9) Click on **Next**, and give your graph and your axes appropriate names. Then click on **Finish**.

10) You will need to modify your graph. You can click on the Legend box, and delete this. You should double click on one of the bars, and in the **Format Data Series** dialog box, click on **Options**, and set your gap width to 0. You will probably also want to resize your chart area. If you need more specific instructions, look back in Chapter 2, and follow the appropriate instructions in section 2-3.

11) When you are done, your probability distribution should look similar to the one below.

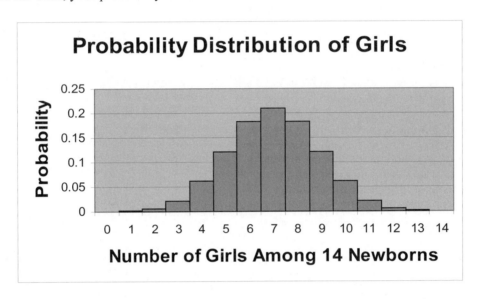

MEAN, VARIANCE AND STANDARD DEVIATION

We can compute the mean, variance and standard deviation of a probability distribution according to formulas 4 – 1, 4 – 3 and 4 – 4 in your book. To use Excel to work with these formulas, follow the steps below. The work below assumes that your x values are in column A, starting in cell A2, and that your probabilities are in column B, starting in cell B2. If your data is in a different location, you should make adjustments as necessary to the specific cell information shown below.

1) In cell D1, type in: x * P(x)

2) In cell D2, type in the following formula: = A2 * B2. This tells Excel to multiply the random variable in cell A2 by its associated probability in cell B2. After pressing **Enter**, you should see a 0 in cell D2, since both values being multiplied are 0.

3) Position your cursor back in cell D2. Then use the fill handle to copy the formula down through cell D16.

4) Formula 4-1 tells us that we need to add these products up. Position your cursor in cell C17, and type "Sum".

5) Position your cursor in cell D17, and click on the **Summation** icon in the toolbar. Notice that the formula: =SUM(D2:D16) appears in cell D17, and the column of numbers directly above this cell is selected. Press **Enter.** You should now see the value 6.993 in cell D 17. This is the mean of the probability distribution.

6) Move to cell C19, and type the word "Mean". In cell C20, type "Variance", and in cell C21, type in "Std.Dev."

7) Move to cell D19 and enter the formula: =$D$17. Notice that this is an absolute address. When you press **Enter**, you should see the value for the mean in cell D19.

8) To compute the variance, we will use Formula 4-3. Position your cursor in cell E1, and type in the formula: + x^2*P(x).

9) Move your cursor to cell E2, and type in the formula: = A2^2*B2. Then press **Enter**. This formula takes the value in cell A2, squares it, and then multiplies it by the value in cell B2.

10) Reposition your cursor in cell E2, and use the fill handle to fill the column down through E16.

11) Position your cursor in cell E17, and click on the summation icon in the toolbar. You should see the formula: =SUM(E2:E16) appear in cell E17. Press **Enter**, and you will see the value 52.467.

X Microsoft Excel - Book1

File Edit View Insert Format Tools Data Window DDXL

Arial   10   **B** *I* <u>U</u>

J20 =

	A	B	C	D	E
1	x	P(x)		x * P(X)	x^2*P(x)
2	0	0		0	0
3	1	0.001		0.001	0.001
4	2	0.006		0.012	0.024
5	3	0.022		0.066	0.198
6	4	0.061		0.244	0.976
7	5	0.122		0.61	3.05
8	6	0.183		1.098	6.588
9	7	0.209		1.463	10.241
10	8	0.183		1.464	11.712
11	9	0.122		1.098	9.882
12	10	0.061		0.61	6.1
13	11	0.022		0.242	2.662
14	12	0.006		0.072	0.864
15	13	0.001		0.013	0.169
16	14	0		0	0
17			Sum	6.993	52.467
18					
19			Mean	6.993	
20			Variance	3.564951	
21			Std. Dev	1.888108	

12) Position your cursor in cell D20 and type in the formula: =$E$17-$D$17^2. This will take the sum of your products and subtract the square of the mean from this sum. This corresponds to Formula 4-3 found in your book.

13) Now position your cursor in cell D21, and type in the following formula: =SQRT($D$20). This will take the square root of the variance, which will produce your standard deviation.

EXPECTED VALUE

Notice that the value that you computed in your worksheet for the summation of the products of your random variables and their corresponding probabilities can also be called the expected value of a discrete random variable.

TO PRACTICE THESE SKILLS

You can apply these technology skills by working on the following exercises. Make sure you save your work using a file name that is indicative of the material contained in your worksheets.

1) Enter the data from exercise 5 in Section 4-2 Basic Skills and Concepts in your textbook. Following the general procedures in the previous tutorial, use Excel, and the appropriate formulas to find the mean and standard deviation for this data.

2) Copy the work that you did for exercise 1 into another worksheet. Replace your P(x) values with the data in exercise 8 from Section 4-2 Basic Skills and Concepts in your textbook. The other values in your worksheet should be automatically updated to reflect this new information.

3) You can continue practicing the skills reviewed in this section by working on exercises 9 and 10 from Section 4-2 Basic Skills and Concepts in your textbook.

SECTION 4-3: BINOMIAL PROBABILITY DISTRIBUTIONS

Binomial variables take on only two values. One of these values is generally designated as a "success" and the other a "failure." We typically see the probability of a "success" denoted by the letter p and the probability of failure denoted by the letter q. The sum of p and q must equal one, since success or failure are the only possible outcomes.

Suppose we consider a binomial distribution where p = .65 and there are 15 trials. Since there are 15 trials, we know that the random variable can take on the values between 0 and 15 inclusive.

Begin your work in a new worksheet. You may want to name this worksheet something like "Bin. Dist", to indicate that you are creating a binomial distribution.

To enter the column of random variables into Excel:

1) Enter a title for the column representing the random variable in cell A1. (If we knew what the random variable represented, we should use a suitable name, otherwise, we will use "x".)

2) In cell A2, type in the value 0, since this is the first value of the random variable. Press **Enter**.

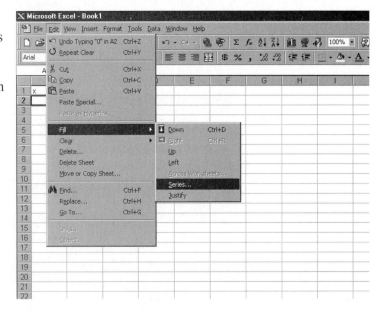

3) Reposition your cursor in cell A2. (Note: In order to activate the fill feature, you **must** move out of the cell where your first value is typed, and then move back to it.) From the command bar, click on **Edit, Fill,** and then click on **Series.**

4) You will see the **Series** dialog box open. (This box is shown on the next page.)

5) Make sure that the bubble in front of **Columns** is checked.

6) Make sure that **Linear** is selected under **Type**.

7) Make sure that the **Step value** is set at 1.

8) Type in 15 for the **Stop value**, since there are 15 trials in the experiment.

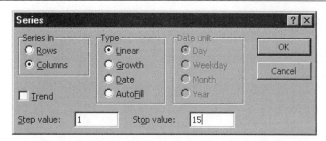

9) Click on **OK**. You should now see the whole numbers from 0 to 15 in column A.

10) Move to column B and type "P(x)" in cell B1. Press **Enter**. Your cursor should now be in cell B2.

11) In the command bar, click on **Insert**, and then click on **Function**. Notice the symbol preceding **Function** can also be found on the menu bar. You may activate this dialog box by clicking on this icon in the menu bar.

12) Select the category **Statistical.** Under **Function,** click on **BINOMDIST**. Then click on **OK**.

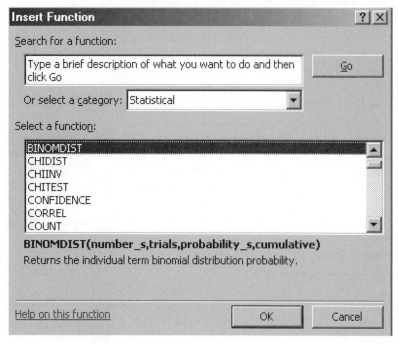

13) You will now see the **BINOMDIST** (Binomial Distribution) Input box. You need to complete the dialog box as follows:

a) **Number_s** refers to the number of successes. You want to enter the cell address where this information is stored. Since we began our values for x in cell A2, we type in A2.
b) **Trials** refers to the total number of trials. Type in 15.
c) **Probability_s** refers to the probability of a success. For this experiment, type in the value .65.
d) **Cumulative** will list the cumulative probabilities. Since we do not want these at this time, type in "False."

e) Click on **OK.**

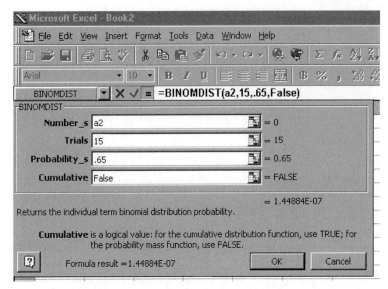

14) You will now see the probability of getting exactly 0 successes in 15 trials if the probability or success is .65. This value may be written in exponential notation. You can reformat the column to show the number with more decimal places.

15) With cell B2 activated, you can use the fill handle to fill in the remaining values in the table.

16) You can likewise create a column showing the cumulative probabilities. In your table, type "P(X<=x)" in cell C1. This represents the probability that X is less than or equal to x, where x refers to the corresponding random variable in column A.

	A	B	C
1	x	P(x)	P(X<=x)
2	0	0.0000001449	0.0000001449
3	1	0.0000040361	0.0000041809
4	2	0.0000524687	0.0000566497
5	3	0.0004222484	0.0004788981
6	4	0.0023525267	0.0028314248
7	5	0.0096117520	0.0124431768
8	6	0.0297506611	0.0421938379
9	7	0.0710372928	0.1132311308
10	8	0.1319264010	0.2451575318
11	9	0.1905603570	0.4357178887
12	10	0.2123386835	0.6480565722
13	11	0.1792469406	0.8273035128
14	12	0.1109623918	0.9382659046
15	13	0.0475553108	0.9858212154
16	14	0.0126167151	0.9984379305
17	15	0.0015620695	1.0000000000

17) Follow the steps above to access the **BINOMDIST** (Binomial Probability Distribution) Input box. The information entered will be the same, except that you will type in "True" in **cumulative.**

18) Again, use the fill handle to copy the function down through cell C17. Notice that cell C17 shows a value equivalent to 1. This should make sense to you, in that the sum of the probabilities in a probability distribution must add to 1.

TO PRACTICE THESE SKILLS

You can apply these technology skills by working on the following exercises. Make sure you save your work using a file name that is indicative of the material contained in your worksheets.

1) Read exercise 27 from Section 4-3 Basic Skills and Concepts in your textbook. Use Excel to set up the probability distribution for this exercise. Before beginning your work in Excel, make sure you clearly identify what the values for your random are, and what value you should use for the probability of "success." Create a column representing the cumulative probabilities. Use your table to answer the question asked in the textbook.

2) Read exercise 28 from Section 4-3 Basic Skills and Concepts in your textbook. Use Excel to set up the probability distribution for this exercise. Create a column representing the cumulative probabilities. Use your table to answer the questions asked.

3) For additional practice, you can work on exercises 29 through 33 from Section 4-3 Basic Skills and Concepts in your textbook. For each problem, you should first generate the entire probability distribution, as well as the column containing the cumulative probabilities.

SECTION 4-4: MEAN, VARIANCE, AND STANDARD DEVIATION FOR BINOMIAL DISTRIBUTION

Although you can use the formulas presented in section 4-2 to compute the mean, variance and standard deviation for the binomial distribution, there are easier formulas to work with for this particular distribution.

- You can find the mean by multiplying the sample size (n) by the probability of success (p).

- You can find the standard deviation by taking the square root of the product formed by multiplying the sample size (n) by the probability of success (p) and the probability of failure (q).

- You should use formulas preceded by the "=" sign when you enter your information into Excel.

Suppose we used the values: n = 14, p = 0.5 and q = 0.5. You can follow the steps below to create a table for this binomial experiment.

1) In cells A1 through A5, type in: "Sample Size," "Probability of Success," "Probability of Failure," "Mean," and "Std. Dev."

2) In cell B1 type in 14. In cells B2 and B3, type in 0.5.

3) In cell B4, type in =B1*B2. When you press **Enter**, you should see the value shown in the table below.

4) In cell B5, type in the formula: = sqrt(B1*B2*B3). Pressing **Enter** should return the value shown in the table below.

Sample Size	14
Probability of Success	0.5
Probability of Failure	0.5
Mean	7
Std. Dev	1.870829

TO PRACTICE THESE SKILLS

Once you have the table from above set up in a worksheet, you can change the values for sample size, probability of success and probability of failure. Your values for the mean and standard deviation should be automatically updated. You can copy this table, paste it in other cells of your worksheet, and then change the numbers in the copy of the table for a different problem.

1) Create a table similar to the one above, but using the data from exercise 5 from Section 4-4 Basic Skills and Concepts in your textbook. To complete part b, you want to compute the values that are 2 standard deviations above and below the mean. Add lines to your table which will use the numbers generated to compute the minimum usual value ($\mu - 2\sigma$) and the maximum usual value ($\mu + 2\sigma$).

2) Copy the table you created in exercise 1, and change the sample size and probabilities of success and failure to complete exercise 7 in your textbook.

3) Copy the table again, and change the sample size and probabilities of success and failure to complete exercise 11 in your textbook.

SECTION 4-5: CREATING A POISSON DISTRIBUTION

In a Poisson distribution, the random variable x is the number of occurrences of the event in an interval. The interval can be time, distance, area, volume, or some similar unit.

Using the example on **World War II Bombs** from section 4-5 in your text, we can generate a table similar to Table 4-4 in your book, showing the probabilities that a region was hit 0, 1, 2, 3, 4 or 5 times. In this example, the computed mean is 0.929.

1) In cell A1, type in "x."

2) In cell A2, type in 0, and press **Enter.**

3) Reposition your cursor in cell A2, and click on **Edit, Fill, Series**.

4) In the **Series** dialog box, click on **Columns**, **Linear**, and enter a step value of 1 and stop value of 5. Then click on **OK.**

5) In cell B1, type in "P(x)."

6) In cell B2, click on **Insert**, **Function**, or click on the function icon (*fx*)on the menu bar. Click on **Statistical** in the **Category** box, and **POISSON** in the **Function** box. Then click on **OK.**

7) In the input box following **x**, type in A2 since this is where the first random variable is located.

8) In the input box following **Mean**, type in 0.929.

9) In the **Cumulative** box, type in "**False."**

10) Click on **OK**. You will now see the probability that a randomly selected region with an area of .25 square kilometers was hit exactly zero times. To match the results in the book, you can format your column to show 3 decimal places.

11) Using the fill handle, fill in the remaining cells.

12) Now suppose we want to use this probability to compute the Expected Number of Regions as found in Table 4-4 in your textbook. In cell C1, type in "Expected Number of Regions." To have the text "wrap" to fit in to the formatted cell width, click on **Format, Cell,** then click on the **Alignment** tab, and click on **Wrap Text**.

13) Move to cell C2. We want to multiply each probability by the total number of regions (576). Enter the formula: = 576 * B2 into cell C2. Then use the fill handle to copy this formula down into the remaining cells. You will notice that some of the numbers generated are slightly different from those in the table in the book. This is because even when Excel is displaying only 3 decimal digits based on our cell formatting, it is using the longer string in computations.

	A	B	C	D
			Expected Number of	
1	x	P(x)	Regions	
2	0	0.395	227.5	
3	1	0.367	211.3	
4	2	0.170	98.2	
5	3	0.053	30.4	
6	4	0.012	7.1	
7	5	0.002	1.3	
8				

TO PRACTICE THESE SKILLS

You can apply these technology skills by working on the following exercises. Make sure you save your work using a file name that is indicative of the material contained in your worksheets.

1) Create a table showing "x" and "P(x)" for exercise 7 from Section 4-5 Basic Skills and Concepts in your textbook.

2) Create a table showing "x", "P(x)" and the "Expected Number" columns for exercise 8 from Section 4-5 Basic Skills and Concepts in your textbook. In this exercise, you first need to compute the mean by dividing 116 by 365.

CHAPTER 5: NORMAL PROBABILITY DISTRIBUTIONS

SECTION 5-1: OVERVIEW

In this chapter we will explore how to compute probabilities for a normal distribution, as well as find specific values if we are given information about the probability for a particular normal distribution. There are essentially five different functions that we can use when exploring normal distributions.

NORMSDIST: This function returns the **standard** normal cumulative distribution for a specified z value.

NORMSINV: This function returns the inverse of the standard normal cumulative distribution for a specified z value.

STANDARDIZE: This function returns a standardized score value for specified values of the random variable, mean and standard deviation.

NORMDIST: This function returns the cumulative normal distribution for specified values of the random variable, mean and standard deviation.

NORMINV: This function returns the inverse of the normal cumulative distribution for specified values for the probability, mean and standard deviation.

SECTION 5-2: WORKING WITH THE STANDARD NORMAL DISTRIBUTION

The first normal distribution presented in your text is the standard normal distribution. This distribution has a mean of 0 and a standard deviation of 1.

FINDING P (0 < Z < A)

Suppose we want to find the probability that a randomly selected z score is between 0 and 1.58. First we must recognize that Excel computes probabilities by determining the total area under the normal distribution **from the left up to a vertical line at a specific value**. Understanding this, we can see that we would first need to compute the probability that our value was less than 1.58, and from that value subtract the probability that our value was less than 0. This would leave us with the area under the curve between 0 and 1.58.

1) In cell A1, type in "x," and in cell B1, type in "P (z<x)" to indicate the probability that a z score is less than the particular x value. This column can be filled in by using the NORMSDIST function from Excel, since Excel gives the total area to the left of a particular value.

2) In cell A2, type in 1.58.

3) Position your cursor in cell B2, and click on the **Function** icon in the toolbar or click on **Insert**, and click on **Function**.

4) In the **Category** box, click on **Statistical**, and in the **Function** box, click on **NORMSDIST**. Make sure you select the name with the "S" for Standard Normal. Then click on **OK** at the bottom of the dialog box.

5) You will now see the **NORMSDIST** (Standard Normal Distribution) dialog box. In the entry box by the **z**, type in "A2" to indicate the cell where your z value is stored.

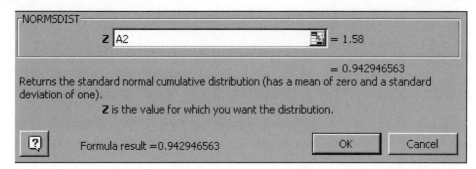

6) Click on **OK**. You should now see the value .942947 displayed in cell B2. This represents the probability that your randomly selected value is less than 1.58. (If you had formatted your column differently, you might have more or less decimal places displayed.)

7) In cell C1, type in "P (0<z<x)" to represent the probability that your score is between 0 and x.

8) In cell C2, enter the formula =B2-0.5. The resulting value is the probability that you will randomly select a value that is between 0 and 1.58. (Since a normal distribution is symmetric about the mean, there is an area of 0.5 to the left of the mean of 0.)

9) Since we now have the formulas entered, we can easily expand our table to compute other probabilities that randomly selected values will fall between 0 and some value greater than 0. In column A, type in 1.2, and 2.3. Move to cell B2 and C2, and use the fill handle to fill in the remainder of the table.

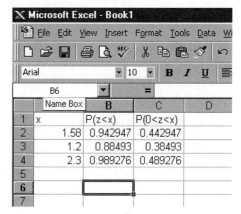

FINDING P (A < Z < B)

Suppose we want to find the probability that a randomly selected score is between 1.2 and 2.3. We can use the **NORMSDIST** function to find the P (z < 1.2) and P (z < 2.3). We can then set up a formula that would subtract the values P (z < 2.3) – P (z < 1.2) to find the desired probability. Using the values from the above table, we should end up with a value of .104346

FINDING P (A < Z < 0) WHEN A IS NEGATIVE

Suppose we want to find the probability that a randomly selected score is greater than -1.3 but less than 0. We can use the **NORMSDIST** function to find P (z < -1.3). Since we know that P (z<0) = .5 by the symmetry of the distribution, we can then subtract the value we produce for P (z<-1.3) from .5 to find the desired probability.

FINDING A SCORE WHEN GIVEN THE PROBABILITY

Let's assume that we are working with thermometers that are normally distributed with a mean of 0 degrees Celsius and a standard deviation of 1 degree Celsius. Suppose we want to find the 95th percentile. This means that we want the area to the left of our value to be .95.

1) Type "P (z < x)" in cell A1, "x" in cell B1, and .95 in cell A2.

2) Position your cursor in cell B2, and click on the **Function** icon on the toolbar (or click on **Insert, Function**).

3) Click on **Statistical, NORMSINV** in the **Category** and **Function** boxes respectively. Then click on **OK**.

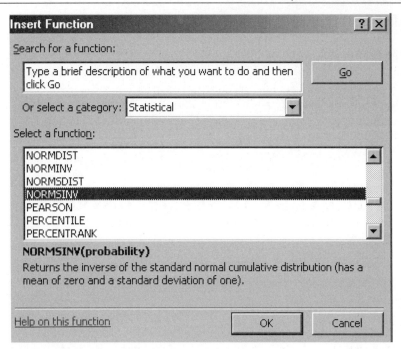

4) Type "A2" in the box by Probability to indicate that the probability is found in this cell, and click on **OK**. You should see a value of 1.644653, which is the score separating the bottom 95 % of the scores from the top 5 %.

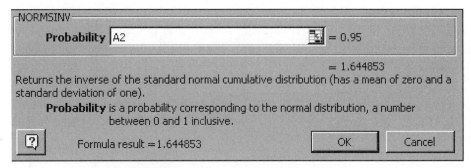

5) You can now enter other areas to the left of the value you want to find, and then find the corresponding z scores by filling the column B with the formula from cell B2.

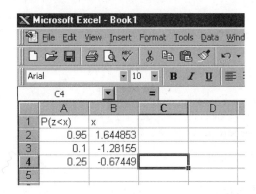

TO PRACTICE THESE SKILLS

1) You can apply the skills you learned in this section to find probabilities by using Excel to complete exercises 9 through 26 and 33 through 36 from Section 5-2 Basic Skills and Concepts in your textbook.

2) You can apply the skills you learned in this section to find scores associated with particular percentiles or probabilities by using Excel to complete exercises 37 through 40 from Section 5-2 Basic Skills and Concepts in your textbook.

SECTION 5-3: APPLICATIONS OF NORMAL DISTRIBUTIONS

STANDARDIZING SCORES

If we are working with a normal distribution which is not a standard normal, we could opt to "standardize" the scores, and then use the techniques for finding probabilities and values as presented in the Standard Normal section.

Let's work with the example for **Jet Ejection Seats** in section 5-3 of your textbook. This example states that women's weights are normally distributed with a mean of 143 lb and a standard deviation of 29 lb. Suppose we want the probability that if a woman is randomly selected, she weighs between 140 and 201 lb.

1) In cell A1, type in "x;" in B1, type in "z;" in C1, type in "Mean;" in D1, type in "SD."

2) In cell A2, type in 201; in C2, type in 143; and in D2, type in 29.

3) Position your cursor in cell B2. Click on the **Function** icon on the toolbar, and click on **Statistical**, **STANDARDIZE.** Then click on **OK**.

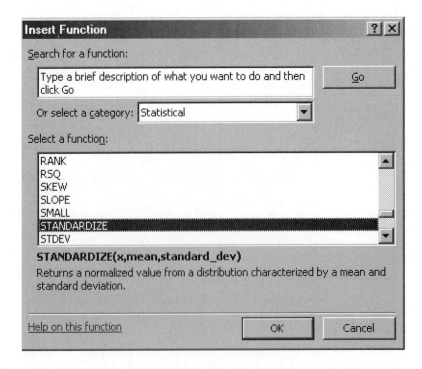

4) In the **Standardize** dialog box, type in "A2" to indicate where the **x** value is stored. Type in "$C$2" to indicate that the **Mean** is an absolute address, and type in "$D$2" to indicate that the **Standard _dev** is also an absolute address. Then click on **OK**.

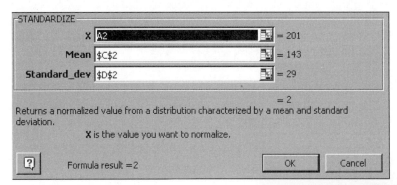

5) The value produced is the "Standardized score" and represents how many standard deviations the value 201 is away from the mean of 143. You can now use the **NORMSDIST** function to compute probabilities for these z scores, as covered in the previous section.

6) To standardize other scores, type the scores in column A, and use the fill handle to copy the formula down in column B.

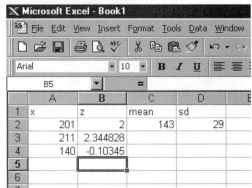

FINDING PROBABILITIES USING THE NORMDIST FUNCTION

We don't need to standardize the scores to find probabilities for non-standard normal distributions.

1) Type in the values 201, 211 and 140 in column A, titling the column "a".

2) Type in "P(x < a)" in cell B1, and type Mean in C1, and Std. Dev in D1.

3) In cell C2, type in 143 for your mean value. In cell D2, type in 29 for your Standard Deviation value. Then position your cursor in cell B2.

4) Click on the **Function** icon from the toolbar, and click on **Statistical, NORMDIST**. Then click on **OK**.

5) In the **NORMDIST** dialog box, type in "A2" for the location of **x**, type in "$C$2" to indicate the cell which contains the mean. Notice that you must use an absolute address in order to ensure that

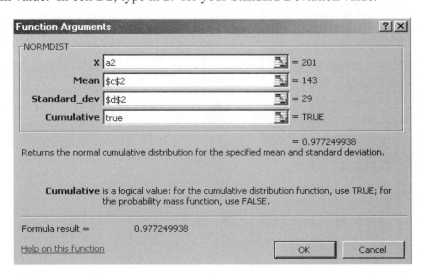

Excel always uses the value in that particular cell. Type in "$D$2" to indicate the cell which contains the Standard deviation. Type "True" for Cumulative. Then click on **OK**.

6) Remember that the resulting value represents the probability that a randomly selected woman weighs less than 201 lb. If you now wanted to find the probability that a randomly selected woman weighed between 143 and 201 lbs, you would need to subtract the area to the left of the mean (.5) from the generated probability. This would produce: P (143 < x < 201) = .47725.

7) You can now create other probabilities P (x < a) by typing in appropriate values in column A and then using the fill handle to create the probabilities in column B. If the value a is above the mean, you can create the value P (mean < x < a) by subtracting .5 from the resulting value.

	A	B	C	D
1	a	P(x<a)	Mean	Std. Dev
2	201	0.97725	143	29
3	211	0.990482		
4	140	0.458804		

8) Suppose we want P (140 < x < 201). We can see in the table above that P(x < 211) = .990482 and that P(x < 140) = .458804. Therefore, P (140 < x < 211) = P(x < 211) – P(x < 140) = .990482 - .458804 = .531679.

FINDING VALUES FROM KNOWN AREAS

Suppose we want to find the 10th percentile for women's weights. Suppose we know the weights are normally distributed with a mean of 143 lb and a standard deviation of 29 lb.

Remember, Excel works with the area to the left of the value that we want.

1) In cell A1, type "P(X < x)". In cell B1 type "x". In cell C1, type "Mean". In cell D1, type "Std. Dev". In cell A2, type in 0.10 to represent that there is an area of 0.10 to the left of the desired score. In cell C2, type in 143. In cell D2, type in 29.

2) Position your cursor in cell B2, and click on the **Function** icon on the toolbar (or click on **Insert, Function**).

3) Click on **Statistical, NORMINV,** and then click on **OK**.

4) In the **NORMINV** dialog box, type in "A2" in the box after **Probability** to indicate this is where the probability is stored. In the **Mean** box, type in the absolute address "$C$2", and in the **Standard_dev** box, type in the absolute

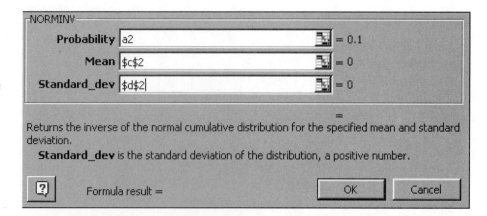

address "$D$2". (Remember, an absolute address entry will not be automatically updated when you fill a column.) Then click on **OK**.

5) The value produced is the score which separates the bottom 10% of the data from the top 90%.

6) In column A, you can now type in other areas to the left of values for percentiles you are interested in, and use the fill handle to fill column B with the formula from B2. Try finding the remaining Deciles.

	A	B	C	D	E
1	P(X<x)	x	Mean	Std. Dev	
2	0.1	105.835027	143	29	
3	0.2	118.5929798			
4	0.3	127.7923709			
5	0.4	135.6529495			
6	0.5	143			
7	0.6	150.3470505			
8	0.7	158.2076291			
9	0.8	167.4070202			
10	0.9	180.164973			

TO PRACTICE THESE SKILLS

Once you have the tables above set up, you can quickly change the values that you input. Excel will automatically update the values in the column containing the formula. To ensure that you can always retrieve the original table that you set up by following the instructions above, it is always best to copy the table to another worksheet before you begin modifying it.

After you complete an exercise, you may want to copy and paste your completed table to another location in your worksheet. After you have copied the table, you should activate the cell where you want your table to begin. Then click on **Edit, Paste Special**, and click in the bubble by the word **Values**. Then click on **OK**. If you activate one of the cells where you had entered a formula originally, you will notice that now only the value shows up. The original formula is no longer active in the copied table. You can go back to the original table to compute the value for the next problem.

1) Try using the table you set up to find Probabilities using the NORMDIST function, and modify the numbers as appropriate to address exercises 1 through 4 from Section 5-3 Basic Skills and Concepts in your textbook.

2) Try using the table you set up to find Values from Known Areas, and modify the numbers as appropriate to address exercises 5 through 8 from Section 5-3 Basic Skills and Concepts in your textbook.

3) Work with the appropriate table, and modify the numbers as appropriate to address exercises 9 through 14 and 17 through 20 from Section 5-3 Basic Skills and Concepts in your textbook.

SECTION 5-4: SAMPLING DISTRIBUTIONS AND ESTIMATORS

This manual does not contain any new material specifically associated with section 5-4. You may find it helpful to review the material on finding the mean from a probability distribution presented backing section 4-2 of this manual.

SECTION 5-5: THE CENTRAL LIMIT THEOREM

In this section, we will use Excel to help us visualize the Central Limit Theorem. We will create a model similar to the one in your textbook, but by using the power of Excel, we can easily consider a higher sample size. We will create a table of 10 columns of randomly generated digits, each column containing 50 values.

Refer back to the instructions in section 3-3 of this manual on "Generating Random Numbers."

1) In your worksheet, type "SSN Digits" in cell A1.

2) Position your cursor in cell A2, and follow the instructions from section 3-3 to create a random number between 0 and 9 in that cell.

3) Use the fill handle to fill this formula to cells B2 through J2.

4) Use the fill handle again to fill a table down to row 51. You should now have a table with 500 digits in it. Your table should look different from others, in that the values in each cell are being randomly generated. Just be aware of this if you are comparing your table to another classmate's table.

5) We want to find the mean of each row. Position your cursor in cell L1 and type in "ROW MEAN."

6) Position your cursor in cell L2, and click on **Insert Function** (or click on the function icon in the toolbar). In the **Category** box, click on **Statistical**, and in the **Function** box, click on **Average.** Click on **OK**.

7) In the input box by Number 1, type in the range "A2:J2," and click on **OK**. In cell L2, you should now see the average of the ten numbers in row 2.

8) You may notice that as you work with your columns and cells, the table of numbers you generated changes. To stabilize the set of data you are working with, highlight the columns containing your values and your means and click on **Edit, Copy.**

9) Move to a new worksheet and position your cursor in cell A1. From the toolbar, click on **Edit, Paste Special**, and then click on the bubble by **Values**. You will now have a stable table, since the cells are representing numbers now rather than formulas. Your pasted table may very well be quite different from the table that you chose to copy! From here out, the copied table will remain stable, as it is no longer associated with the random number generator.

10) Create a Histogram for the 500 digits found in your table. (Refer back to Chapter 2 if necessary.)

11) You should see clearly that your histogram does not appear bell shaped.

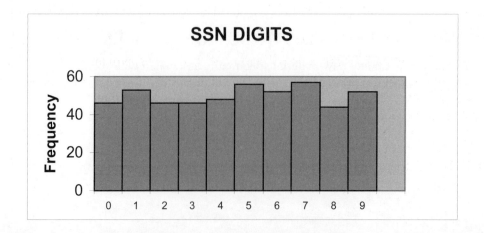

12) Now create a histogram of your 50 sample means.

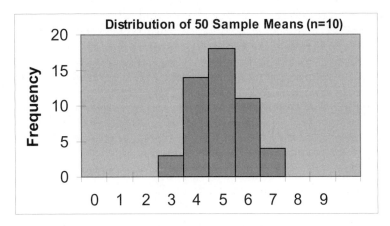

Distribution of 50 Sample Means (n=10)

13) Although this may not look entirely bell shaped, it is definitely moving in that direction. Keep in mind that our sample size is still quite small. If we increased the number of values we used to compute each sample mean, we should find that our distribution of sample means becomes increasingly bell shaped.

Computing Probabilities for Situations Involving the Central Limit Theorem

In section 5-3, we learned how to use the **NORMDIST** function to compute probabilities for non-standard normal distributions. In a situation involving the Central Limit Theorem, we will use the same approach; however we will need to enter the standard deviation as $\sigma/\sqrt{n}$.

TO PRACTICE THESE SKILLS

You can apply the skills you learned in this section by working on the following exercises.

1) Repeat the exercise presented in this section, but using a table with 100 rows of 10 digits. Compare the histograms you create from your new data set to those presented in this section.

2) Many of the exercises in Section 5-5 of your textbook deal with finding probabilities. Use the patterns established in Section 5-3 to complete the odd numbered exercises 1 – 19 from Section 5-5 Basic Skills and Concepts in your textbook. **Notice that when you are looking for the probability involving a mean, you must recognize that the Central Limit applies, and that the standard deviation you must use in generating your probability will be** $\sigma/\sqrt{n}$.

SECTION 5-6: NORMAL DISTRIBUTION AS APPROXIMATION TO BINOMIAL

If we have a binomial distribution where $np \geq 5$ and $nq \geq 5$, we can approximate binomial probability problems by using a normal distribution. The material below helps you see a clear demonstration that this approach will work. We will plot three different binomial probability distributions to see that as the sample size increases, our distribution appears to look more and more like a normal distribution.

In a new worksheet, we will create three binomial probability distributions:

- Let the first distribution have n = 10 and p = 0.5

- Let the second distribution have n = 25 and p = 0.5
- Let the third distribution have n = 50 and p = 0.5

1) Refer back to section 4-3 on Binomial Distributions and create your pairs of columns for the random variable and the associated probabilities in columns A & B; D & E; and G & H.

2) Click on the **Chart** icon, and click on the **Custom Types** tab. Scroll down until you see the **Line-Column** option. Click on this option.

3) Click on **Next**.

4) For your first graph, select the cells containing the probabilities in column B.

5) Click on the **Series** tab, and underneath the **Series** box, click on **Add**. You should see another Series name in the box.

6) Delete the information that is in the **Values** box, and select the probabilities that are in column B.

7) Click on **Next**, and enter the appropriate information for the Chart Title and the axes names.

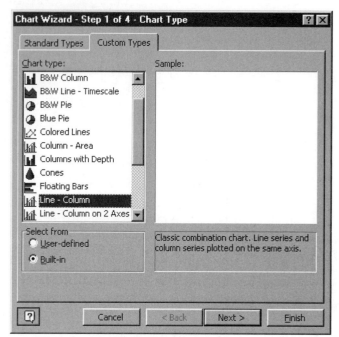

8) Click on **Next**. Choose to insert the chart in a new sheet.

9) Once your chart appears, double click in the **Plot Area**. Click on **Options** in the dialog box, and change your gap size to 0.

10) Repeat this process to create the pictures for the other two binomial distributions. Your pictures should appear as the three shown:

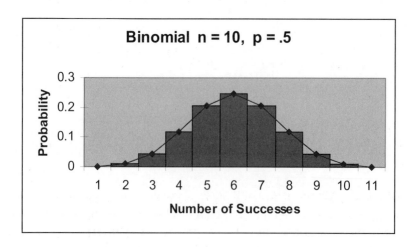

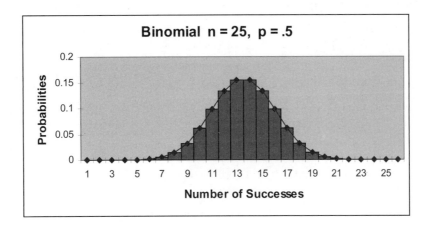

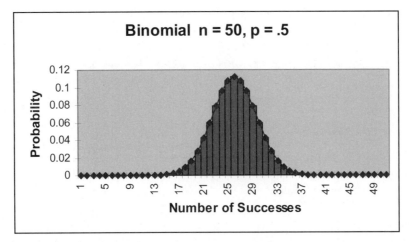

11) What you should notice about each of these successive pictures is that the areas in the bars, which represent the probabilities for each random variable, more closely approximates the area contained under the curve. If you think of the curve as representing a normal curve, than you can clearly see that the binomial probability distribution is more closely approaching a normal distribution.

We can see that the probabilities we find using the normal distribution will closely match those that we can generate from the binomial distribution. To see this clearly, we will use the case of n = 50 and p = 0.5.

1) Using the values in our binomial distribution table, we can find $P(x \geq 30)$ by adding up the probabilities from x = 30 to x = 50. This produces a value of .101319.

2) If we want to use a normal distribution, we will need to compute the mean and standard deviation using the formulas for a binomial distribution. You should find the value for the mean is 25 and the standard deviation is 3.535534.

3) As outlined in section 5-6 of your textbook, we need to use a continuity correction when using the normal distribution to approximate the binomial. Since we want to find the probability of getting a value greater than or equal to 30, we should find $P(x \geq 29.5)$. Use the **NORMDIST** function on Excel. Remember that Excel returns a value that represents the area under the normal distribution curve to the left of the value. In order to find the probability we really want, we will need to subtract this value from 1. The **NORMDIST** function returns a value of 0.898454. Subtracting this value from 1 produces a probability of .101546. Recall that the probability using our binomial information is .101319. If we

were to increase our sample size, we would find that we get even closer approximations when using the normal distribution to approximate the binomial.

TO PRACTICE THESE SKILLS

You can apply the skills you learned in this section by working on the following exercises.

1) Create the picture showing the Line-Column graph for a binomial probability distribution where n = 100 and p = 0.5. Compare your picture to those for n = 10, 25 and 50 found in this section.

2) Use the **NORMDIST** function on Excel, and the continuity correction to find the probabilities for the odd numbered exercises 1 – 7 in Section 5-6 Basic Skills and Concepts in your textbook. To recall how to work with the NORMDIST function, you may want to refer back to instructions found in Section 5-3 of this manual.

3) Use the **BINOMDIST** function on Excel, and, when appropriate, the **NORMDIST** function with the continuity correction to find the probabilities asked for in the odd numbered exercises 9 – 27 from Section 5-6 Basic Skills and Concepts in your textbook. To recall how to work with the BINOMDIST function, you may want to refer back to instructions found in Section 4-3 of this manual.

SECTION 5-7: DETERMINING NORMALITY

Oftentimes we want to know whether the data we are working with is normally distributed. We have already learned how to create histograms for sample data. From our histogram, we can reject normality if the histogram departs dramatically from bell shape.

An alternate way to determine normality is to construct a normal probability plot for the data. In a normal probability plot, the observations in the data set need to be ordered from smallest to largest. These values are then plotted against the expected z scores of the observations calculated under the assumption that the data are from a normal distribution. When the data are normally distributed, a linear trend will result. A nonlinear trend suggests that the data are non-normal.

We can use the **DDXL** Add-In to generate a normal probability plot. We will create a model similar to the **Diet Pepsi** example found in section 5-7 of your book, but using the sample of 36 weights of diet Coke listed in Data Set 1 of Appendix B.

1) Load the data from the CD that comes with your book (COLA.XLS) Copy the column showing the 36 weights of Diet Coke into column A of a new Excel worksheet.

2) Click on **DDXL** on your menu bar.

3) Click on **Charts and Plots**. Click on the down arrow on the Function type box, and click on **Normal Probability Plot.**

4) Click on the pencil icon for **Quantitative Variable**, and enter the range of values for your data. If your column title appears in cell A1, and your data started in cell A2, you range will be entered as "A2:A37".

5) Click on **OK.** You should see the following information on your screen.

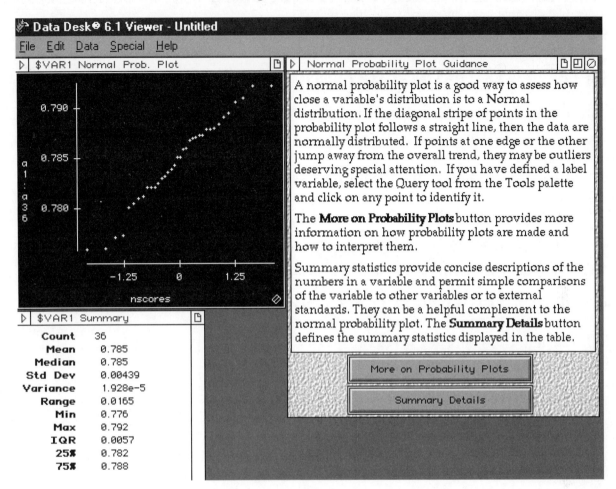

TO PRACTICE THESE SKILLS

You can apply the skills from this section by working with exercises 5, 6, 7 & 8 from section 5-7 Basic Skills and Concepts in your textbook. For each exercise, you should open the file in an Excel workbook from the CD that comes with your book. The file names are listed below:

For exercise 5, Boston Rainfall data is in the file named BOSTRAIN.XLS.
For exercise 6, Head Circumferences data is in the file named HEADCIRC.XLS
For exercise 7, Weights of M&Ms data is in the file named M&M.XLS.
For exercise 8, Water Conductivity data is in the file named EVERGLADE.XLS

CHAPTER 6: ESTIMATES AND SAMPLE SIZES

SECTION 6-1: OVERVIEW

Many times we do not know the value of the parameters that are used to describe a population and need to resort to using information contained in a sample. If we can identify a numerical value that describes the sample, then this value can also be used to estimate the corresponding descriptor for the population. **Confidence intervals** are important in statistics because they allow you to gauge how accurately a sample parameter approximates the same parameter with respect to the population. The confidence interval consists of a range (or interval) of values instead of just a single value. The confidence interval also contains a probability. This probability value tells you the likelihood that you have an interval that actually contains the value of the unknown population parameter. Components of a confidence interval include a lower limit and an upper limit for the parameter under consideration, as well as a probability value.

Excel does not have a built in function that automatically calculates the confidence interval. We will need to rely on some of the functions we have already used in Excel to help us with this process. In addition to exploring this topic with Excel we will make use of the add-in DDXL. This add-in was supplied on the CD that came with your textbook. If you did not load the DDXL add-in or cannot find it on the computer you are working with please go back to Chapter 2, Section 7 and follow the instructions for loading DDXL.

The following list contains an overview of the functions we will be utilizing in this chapter.

CONFIDENCE: Returns the confidence interval for a population mean.
CONFIDENCE (alpha, standard_dev, size) where alpha refers to the significance level used to compute the confidence interval, standard_dev is the population standard deviation for the data range and size is the sample size.

TINV: Returns the inverse of the Student's t-distribution for the specified degrees of freedom.
TINV (probability, deg_freedom) where probability is the probability associated with a two tailed Student's t distribution and deg_freedom is a positive integer indicating the number of degrees of freedom needed to characterize the distribution.

SECTION 6-2: ESTIMATING A POPULATION PROPORTION

Excel does not produce confidence interval estimates for proportions. It will be necessary for us to use the **DDXL** add-in that came as a supplement to your textbook to do this. If you have not loaded **DDXL** please do so now. The instructions for adding this feature to Excel can be found in Chapter 2, Section 7 of this manual. If you are unsure as to whether or not you have already added DDXL check the menu bar in Excel to see if it featured on the menu bar as seen below.

```
File  Edit  View  Insert  Format  Tools  Data  Window  DDXL  Help
```

DETERMINING A CONFIDENCE INTERVAL FOR A POPULATION PROPORTION:

To determine the confidence interval for a population proportion using **DDXL** we will begin by considering the **"Photo Cop" Survey"** results found in the Chapter Problem at the start of Chapter 6.

1) Label cells A1 and A2 as shown in the Excel worksheet on the next page. Enter the number of successes in cell B1 and the number of trials in cell B2.

2) Click on **DDXL**.

3) Highlight **Confidence Intervals** and click.

4) Select **Summ 1 Var Prop Interval** as seen below in the screen on the left.

5) Click on the **pencil icon** for **"num successes"** and enter the cell address B1.

6) Click on the **pencil icon** for **"num trials"** and enter the cell address B2.

7) After completing steps (5) and (6) you should see a screen similar to the one on the right.

8) Click **OK.**

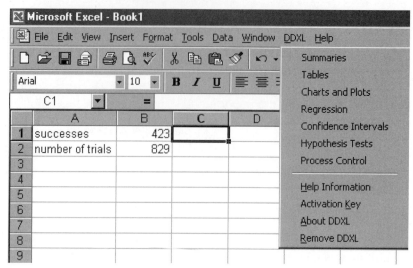

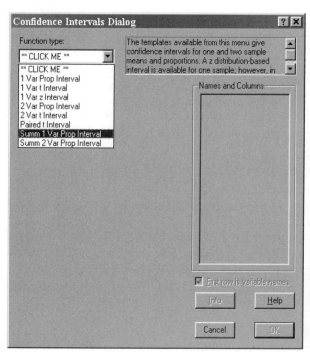

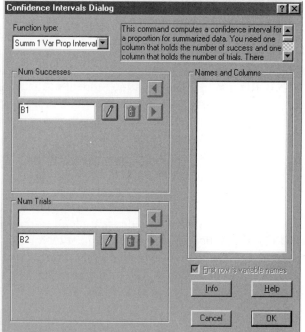

In the dialog box that looks like the one seen on the right

a) Select the appropriate level of confidence, in this case **95%**

b) Click on **Compute Interval**.

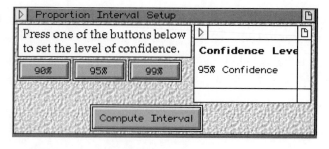

A summary dialog box similar to the one shown on the right displays the confidence interval for the population proportion.

```
$VAR1 Confidence Interval

 Summary Statistics          Interval Results

      n    829              Confidence Interval
  p-hat    0.51
Std Err    0.0174           With 95% Confidence, 0.476 < p < 0.544
     z*    1.96
```

It is possible to **copy and paste your DDXL results** to your Excel worksheet.

1) Click on the title bar of the window you wish to copy into Excel.

2) From the **Edit** menu choose **Copy Window**.

3) Switch to Excel and choose **Paste** from the **Edit** menu or use the **Paste Function** feature.

TO PRACTICE THESE SKILLS

You can practice the technology skills learned in this section by working through the following problems found in your textbook.

1) Use **DDXL** to work through problems 17 and 19 in Section 6-2 Basic Skills and Concepts. Note that the problem asks for the confidence interval as a percentage. DDXL will return a decimal value. You will need to rewrite your results in the appropriate format.

2) Use **DDXL** to work through problem 31 in Section 6-2 Basic Skills and Concepts. Note that you will have to determine the number of successes before you begin.

3) Use **DDXL** to work through problem 37 in Section 6-2 Basic Skills and Concepts.

4) Use the data found in Data Set 19 in appendix B of your textbook or the data file "M&M" found on the CD data disk to work through problem 43 in Section 6-2 Basic Skills and Concepts.

SECTION 6-3: ESTIMATING A POPULATION MEAN: σ KNOWN

The formula for the confidence interval for the population mean when the standard deviation σ is known is

given by $\overline{X} - E < \mu < \overline{X} + E$ where $E = z_{\alpha/2} \cdot \dfrac{\sigma}{\sqrt{n}}$

To determine a confidence interval for the mean in Excel you must know the value for $\overline{X}$ and for σ. These can be found using the built in statistical functions within Excel or from Descriptive Statistics in the Data Analysis Tools.

Begin by entering the data found in Data Set 4 in Appendix B (Body Temperatures of 106 Healthy Adults) into Excel. Use the temperatures taken at 12AM on day 2.

Use the paste function feature of Excel to determine the sample mean and standard deviation.

DETERMINING CONFIDENCE INTERVALS

To find the **confidence interval** we need to use the **Paste Function** feature.

1) Under Function category click on Statistical.

2) Scroll through the list of Function names until you see **CONFIDENCE.** Click on this function name.

3) Click **OK**.

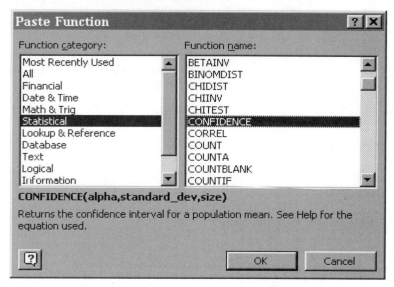

The following dialogue box will appear in the upper left-hand corner of your Excel workbook.

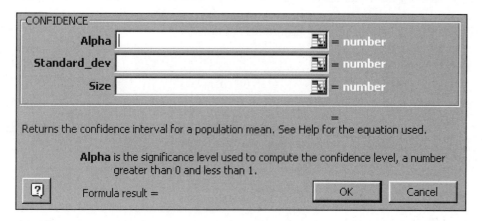

4) Assuming a degree of confidence of 95% we can fill in the information required. Recall that with a degree of confidence of 95%, $\alpha = 0.05$. Enter the standard deviation and the size of the sample. Your worksheet should look similar to the screenshot found on the next page.

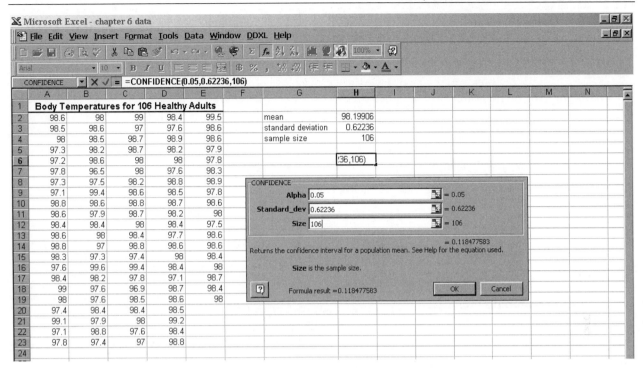

The value returned is called the **margin of error** (or **maximum error**) and is denoted by the letter E in the formula presented at the beginning of this section.

1) Determine the upper confidence interval limit ($\overline{X} + E$) and the lower confidence interval limit ($\overline{X} - E$).

2) Using the general format $\overline{X} - E < \mu < \overline{X} + E$ used to display a confidence interval substitute in the values found in step #1 above.

   a) The lower limit is found using the formula =(H2-H6)
   b) The upper limit is found by using the formula =(H2+H6)

3) This will give you a confidence interval $98.08° < \mu < 98.32°$.

CONFIDENCE INTERVALS WITH DDXL

You may also determine a confidence interval for a population mean when σ is known using the DDXL add-in. It is recommended that you try both methods (Excel functions and the DDXL add-in). To use DDXL to determine a confidence interval it will be necessary to enter your data in a single column. You can move the data you have already entered into your Excel worksheet into one column by following the instructions found in chapter 1 in Section 3 under "Dropping and Dragging."

1) Click on **DDXL.**

2) Highlight **Confidence Intervals** and click.

3) Select **1 Var z Interval**.

4) Click on the **pencil icon** and enter the range of data (for example A2:A107).

5) Click **OK.**

In the dialog box that looks like the one seen on the right

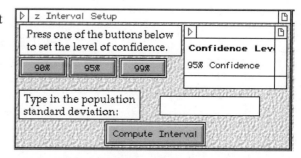

  a) Select the appropriate level of confidence, in this case **95%**.
  b) Enter the standard deviation for the sample.
  c) Click on **Compute Interval**.

A summary dialog box similar to the one shown on the right displays the confidence interval for the population proportion.

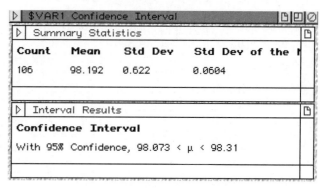

As with our previous DDXL problem, it is possible to copy and paste your results to your Excel worksheet.

TO PRACTICE THESE SKILLS

The problems following Section 6-4 in this manual will help you to practice the technology skills introduced in Sections 6-3 & 6-4 of this chapter. Use both Excel and DDXL when working through these problems in order to become familiar with both.

SECTION 6-4: ESTIMATING A POPULATION MEAN: σ NOT KNOWN

In this section we will present a method for determining a confidence interval estimate for the population mean, μ without the requirement that σ be known. The student *t* distribution is used to estimate the population mean. The sample confidence interval is $\overline{X} - E < \mu < \overline{X} + E$ where $E = t_{\alpha/2} \cdot \dfrac{s}{\sqrt{n}}$.

Note that the sample standard deviation *s*, replaces the population standard deviation σ in the formula. To determine the small sample confidence intervals or the population mean with Excel, use the **TINV** function to determine the appropriate *t* **values.**

Use the data found in Data Set 4 in Appendix B (Body Temperatures of 106 Healthy Adults) already entered into Excel. These are the temperatures taken at 12AM on day 2. You can copy this data to a blank worksheet. Copy or determine the sample mean and standard deviation.

We will use this information to determine

- a) The margin of error *E*.
- b) The confidence interval for μ.

These can be determined easily using the built in functions in Excel.

DETERMINING CONFIDENCE INTERVAL USING A T DISTRIBUTION

To determine the *t* **value** we will follow the same method used to find the confidence interval outline earlier in this section:

To find the **TINV confidence interval** we need to use the **Paste Function** feature.

5) Under **Function** category click on **Statistical.**

6) Scroll through the list of **Function** names until you see **TINV.** Click on this function name.

7) Click **OK.**

The following dialogue box will appear in the upper left hand corner of your Excel workbook.

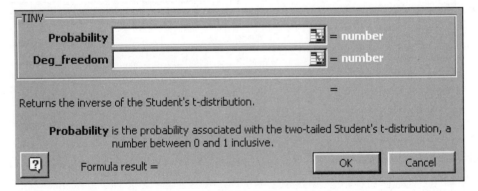

Assuming a degree of confidence of 95% we can fill in the information required. Recall that with a degree of confidence of 95%, the probability = 0.05, the deg_freedom is 105.

Your worksheet should look similar to the screen shown on the next page.

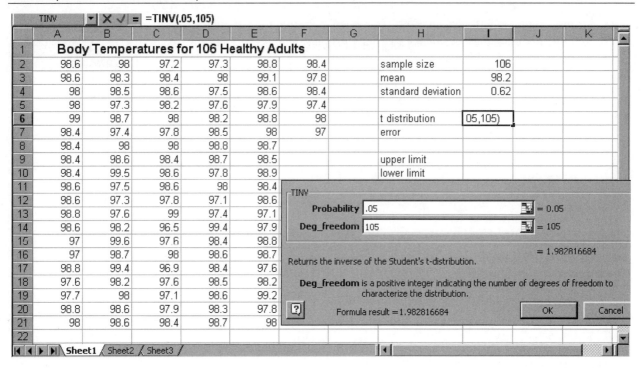

You can complete the information on the worksheet using the same procedures outlined for the confidence interval. This will give you the information presented below. While the values may be slightly different than those presented in your textbook this is primarily due to rounding.

	A	B	C	D	E	F	G	H	I
1	Body Temperatures for 106 Healthy Adults								
2	98.6	98	97.2	97.3	98.8	98.4		sample size	106
3	98.6	98.3	98.4	98	99.1	97.8		mean	98.2
4	98	98.5	98.6	97.5	98.6	98.4		standard deviation	0.62
5	98	97.3	98.2	97.6	97.9	97.4			
6	99	98.7	98	98.2	98.8	98		t distribution	1.983
7	98.4	97.4	97.8	98.5	98	97		error	0.119
8	98.4	98	98	98.8	98.7				
9	98.4	98.6	98.4	98.7	98.5			upper limit	98.30
10	98.4	99.5	98.6	97.8	98.9			lower limit	98.07
11	98.6	97.5	98.6	98	98.4				
12	98.6	97.3	97.8	97.1	98.6				
13	98.8	97.6	99	97.4	97.1				
14	98.6	98.2	96.5	99.4	97.9				
15	97	99.6	97.6	98.4	98.8				
16	97	98.7	98	98.6	98.7				
17	98.8	99.4	96.9	98.4	97.6				
18	97.6	98.2	97.6	98.5	98.2				
19	97.7	98	97.1	98.6	99.2				
20	98.8	98.6	97.9	98.3	97.8				
21	98	98.6	98.4	98.7	98				

CONFIDENCE INTERVALS WITH DDXL

You may also determine a confidence interval for a population mean when σ is not known using DDXL. It is recommended that you try both methods (the Excel functions and DDXL). To use DDXL to determine a confidence interval when σ is not known follow the instructions outlined in the previous section. Choose the **1 Var t Interval** rather than the I Var z Interval.

The following result will be returned:

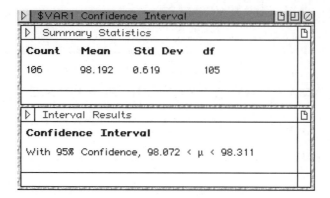

TO PRACTICE THESE SKILLS

The following problems will help you to practice the technology skills introduced in Sections 6-3 & 6-4 of this chapter. Use both Excel and DDXL when working through these problems in order to become familiar with both.

1) Use the data found in Data Set 2 in Appendix B of your textbook or the data file "PARENTH" found on the CD data disk that accompanies your book to work through problem 16 in Section 6-4 Basic Skills and Concepts.

2) Use Excel and DDXL to work through problem 22 in Section 6-4 Basic Skills and Concepts.

3) Use Excel and DDXL to work through problem 23 in Section 6-4 Basic Skills and Concepts.

CHAPTER 7: HYPOTHESIS TESTING

SECTION 7-1: OVERVIEW

This chapter will look at the statistical process used for testing a claim made about population. Chapter 6 used sample statistics to estimate population parameters; in this chapter we will use sample statistics to test hypotheses made about population parameters. While Excel has many built in statistical analysis tools available, it does not have a tool for hypothesis tests for the mean. We will use the DDXL add-in for the various hypotheses tests we will perform in this chapter.

SECTION 7-2: TESTING A CLAIM ABOUT A PROPORTION

Once you understand the different components of a hypothesis test (as outlined in your textbook) you will be ready to use those components to test claims made about population proportions. We will utilize the DDXL add in to perform a z test of the hypothesis for a proportion.

Z TEST FOR ONE VARIABLE PROPORTION TEST:

In the Chapter Problem found at the beginning of Chapter 7 it was noted, "of 880 randomly selected drivers, 56% admitted that they run red lights." We will test the claim that the majority of all American drivers run red lights. This problem is outlined in the **survey of Drivers** example found in Section 7-3 of your textbook.

1) Begin by entering the number of drivers surveyed and the population proportion that admitted to running a red light into Excel: ($n = 880$ $\hat{p} = 0.56$)

2) DDXL will require the number of trials (n) and the number of successes. To determine the number of successes multiply $880 \cdot 0.56 = 492.8$. Round the 492.8 up to 493 and enter this value into your Excel worksheet.

	A	B
1	n	880
2	Proportion	0.56
3		
4	trials	880
5	successes	493

3) Select **DDXL** from the tool bar, scroll down to **Hypothesis Tests** and click.

4) From the **Hypothesis Tests Dialog** box select **Summ 1 Var Prop Test** from Function type.

5) Click on the pencil icon for **Num Successes** and enter the cell address for the number of drivers who admitted to running a red light. Be sure to enter the cell address rather than the actual number of number of drivers.

6) Click on the pencil icon for **Num Trials** and enter the cell address of total number of people surveyed.

7) Click **OK**.

8) This will open a dialog box that will require additional information. Complete each of the four steps in the dialog box as outlined on the following page.

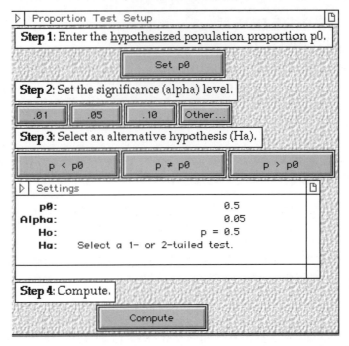

a) **Step 1:** Click on **"Set pθ"**. We will enter the hypothesized test proportion found within the example ($p = 0.5$). Enter the value in the appropriate spot and click **OK.**

b) **Step 2:** Set the **significance level** by clicking on the appropriate value. In this case use a significance level of 0.05.

c) **Step 3:** Select the alternative hypothesis. In this problem the null hypothesis states H_0: $p = 0.5$. Therefore the alternative hypothesis is H_1: $p > 0.5$. Choose p > pθ.

d) **Step 4:** Click on **Compute.**

9) **DDXL** presents the following results that include the test statistic, the P – value and a conclusion to reject the null hypothesis.

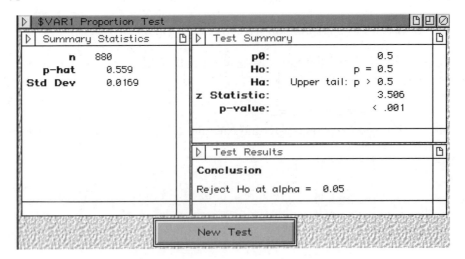

TO PRACTICE THESE SKILLS

You can apply the technology skills learned in this section by working on the following problems.

1) To practice testing claims about proportions work through problems 3, 7, 13 and 15 found in the Basic Skills and Concepts for Section 7-3 of your textbook.

2) Use Data Set 19 to work through problem 19 in the Basic Skills and Concepts for Section 7-3 of your textbook. This problem gives you an opportunity to start with actual data to test a claim about proportions.

SECTION 7-3: TESTING A CLAIM ABOUT A MEAN: σ KNOWN

In this section we test claims made about a population mean μ, and we assume that the population standard deviation σ is known. Begin by opening the Excel file that contains the Body Temperature data we worked with in the last chapter. This data can also be found in Data Set 4 in Appendix B. We will test the common belief that the mean body temperature of healthy adults is equal to 98.6°

TESTING CLAIMS ABOUT A POPULATION MEAN μ (σ KNOWN)

1) Select **DDXL** from the tool bar, scroll down to **Hypothesis Tests** and click.

2) From the **Hypothesis Tests Dialog** box select **I Var z Test** from Function type.

3) Click on the pencil icon and list the range of cells that include your data.

4) Click **OK**.

5) Complete each of the four steps listed in the dialog box shown below. These steps are outlined on the next page.

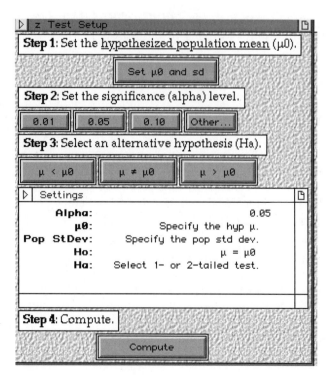

a) **Step 1:** Click on **"Set $\mu\theta$ and sd."** The hypothesized mean is 98.6^0. When working with this data in the previous chapter we determined the standard deviation to be 0.62^0. Enter the values for the hypothesized mean and standard deviation in the appropriate spot and click **OK.**

b) **Step 2:** Set the **significance level** by clicking on the appropriate value. In this case use a significance level of 0.05.

c) **Step 3:** Select the **alternative hypothesis**. In this problem the null hypothesis states that the mean body temperature of healthy adults is equal to 98.6^0. Therefore the alternative hypothesis states that the mean temperature is not equal to 98.6^0. Choose $\mu \neq \mu\theta$.

d) **Step 4:** Click on **Compute**.

6) DDXL presents the following results that include the test statistic, the P – value and a conclusion to reject the null hypothesis.

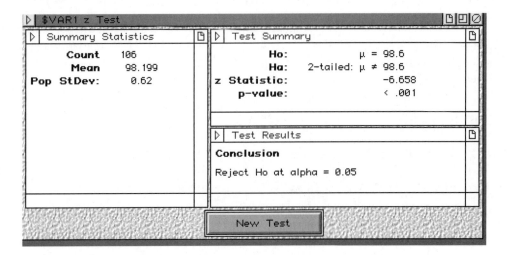

TO PRACTICE THESE SKILLS

You can practice the skills learned in this section by working through the following problems.

1) Use Data Set 5 found in Appendix B or in the data file CIGARET.xls to work through problem 11 in the Basic Skills and Concepts for Section 7-4 of your textbook.

2) Use Data Set 3 found in Appendix B or in the data file HEADCIRC.xls to work through problem 12 in the Basic Skills and Concepts for Section 7-4 of your textbook.

SECTION 7- 4: TESTING A CLAIM ABOUT A MEAN: σ NOT KNOWN

In this section we turn our attention to testing claims made about a population mean μ when the population standard deviation σ is not known. We will use the Student t distribution rather than the normal distribution used in the preceding section where σ was known. We will rely on the DDXL add-in to perform a t test of the hypothesis of the mean. This test compares the observed t test statistic to the point of the t distribution that corresponds to the test's chosen α level.

TESTING CLAIMS ABOUT A POPULATION MEAN μ (WITH σ NOT KNOWN):

Begin by entering the data found in the **Body Temperatures** example in Section 7-5. We will use this data and a significance level of $\alpha = 0.05$ to test the claim that these body temperatures come from a population with a mean that is less than 98.6^0F.

1) Select **DDXL** from the tool bar, scroll down to **Hypothesis Tests** and click.

2) From the **Hypothesis Tests Dialog** box select **I Var t Test** from Function type.

3) Click on the pencil icon and list the range of cells that include your data.

4) Click **OK**.

5) Complete each of the four steps listed in the dialog box as outlined below.

   a) **Step 1:** Click on **"Set μθ"**. Enter the values for the hypothesized population mean (H_o: $\mu = 98.6^0$F) and click **OK**.

   b) **Step 2:** Set the **significance level** by clicking on the appropriate value. In this case use a significance level of $\alpha = 0.05$.

   c) **Step 3:** Select the **alternative hypothesis**. In this problem the alternative hypothesis states that the average body temperature is less than 98.6^0F (H_1: $\mu < 98.6^0$F). Therefore we choose $\mu < \mu\theta$.

   d) **Step 4:** Click on **Compute.**

6) **DDXL** presents the following results that include the test statistic, the P – value and a conclusion to fail to reject the null hypothesis.

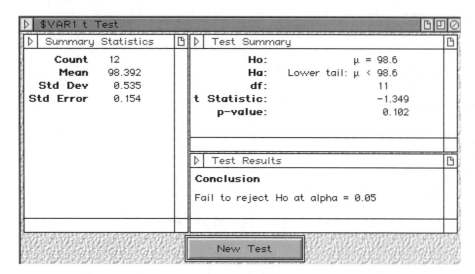

TO PRACTICE THESE SKILLS

You can practice the technology skills learned in this section by working on the following problems.

1) Use Data Set 14 found in Appendix B or combine the data found in the files CLANCY.xls, ROWLING.xls, and TOLSTOY.xls into a single worksheet in order to work through problem 13 in the Basic Skills and Concepts for Section 7-5 of your textbook.

2) Use Data Set 10 found in Appendix B or in the data file WEATHER.xls to work through problem 15 in the Basic Skills and Concepts for Section 7-5 of your textbook.

3) To work with sample data, try working through problem 27 in the Basic Skills and Concepts for Section 7-5 of your textbook.

CHAPTER 8: INFERENCES FROM TWO SAMPLES

SECTION 8-1: OVERVIEW

In Chapters 6 and 7 we used sample data to construct confidence interval estimates of population parameters and to test hypotheses about certain population parameters. In each case we used one sample to form an inference about one population. In this chapter we will turn our attention to confidence intervals and hypothesis tests for comparing two sets of sample data. In this chapter we will utilize the capabilities if Excel as well as the DDXL add-in to test the hypothesis made about two population means.

- the Data Analysis **z-Test: Two Samples for Means.**

- the DDXL add-in Hypothesis Tests: **2 Var t Test**

t-Test: Paired Samples for Means
This analysis tool and its formula perform a paired two-sample student's t-test to determine whether a sample's means are distinct. This t-test form does not assume that the variances of both populations are equal. You can use a paired test when there is a natural pairing of observations in the samples, such as when a sample group is tested twice — before and after an experiment.

F Test Two Samples for Variances
This analysis tool performs a two-sample F-test to compare two population variances and to determine whether the two population variances are equal. It returns the p value of the one tailed F statistic, based on the hypothesis that array 1 and array 2 have the same variance.

t-Test: Two Samples Assuming Equal Variances
This test calculates a two sample Student t Test. The test assumes that the variance in each of the two groups is equal. The output includes both one tailed and two tailed critical values.

t-Test: Two Samples Assuming Unequal Variances.
This test calculates a two sample Student t Test. The test allows the variances in the two groups to be unequal. The output includes both one tailed and two tailed critical values.

SECTION 8-2: INFERENCES ABOUT TWO PROPORTIONS

When using sample data to compare two population proportions we will use DDXL and the **Summ 2 Var Prop Test.**   Since we are comparing two population proportions we will need to enter the number of successes as well as the number of trials for both Sample 1 and Sample 2 into Excel.

Enter the information presented in the **Racial Profiling** Example found in Section 8-2 of your textbook into Excel:

	A	successes	trials
1		successes	trials
2	black drivers	24	200
3	white drivers	147	1400

Use the following steps and a 0.05 significance level to test the claim that the proportion of black drivers stopped by the police is greater than the proportion on white drivers who are stopped.

DDXL – SUMM 2 VAR PROP TEST

1) Click on **DDXL** and choose **Hypotheses Tests** and **Summ 2 Var Prop Test**.

2) In the Hypothesis test dialog box click on the pencil icons and enter the appropriate cell address for the number of success as well as the address for the number of trials for the black drivers. Repeat this process to enter the cell addresses for the number of successes and the number of trials for the white drivers.

3) Click **OK**.

4) Follow these steps in the **Proportion Test Setup** dialog box:

   a) **Step 1:** This step is optional so you can skip it or set the difference at 0 (since we will only be testing claims that $p_1 = p_2$).

   b) **Step 2:** For this example set the significance level at 0.05.

   c) **Step 3:** Select the appropriate alternative hypothesis, in this case **p1 – p2 > p.**

   d) **Step 4:** Click on **Compute**.

5) DDXL returns the following results. Compare these results with those found in your textbook. DDXL returns the value for test statistic, the p –value as well as the conclusion to reject the null hypothesis.

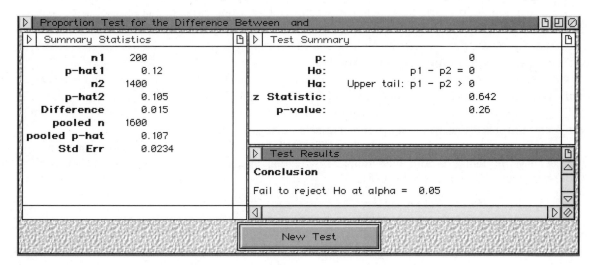

DDXL - CONFIDENCE INTERVALS FOR PROPORTION PAIRS

We can construct a confidence interval estimate of the difference between population proportions for the sample date presented in the **Racial Profiling** example using DDXL.

1) Click on **DDXL**, select **Confidence Interval – Summ 2 Var Prop Interval.**

2) In the dialog box click on each of the pencil icons and enter the appropriate cell addresses for the number of successes and trials for black drivers. Repeat this process for the number of successes and trials for the white drivers.

3) Click **OK**.

4) A dialog box will open in order for you to set the appropriate confidence level. In this case we choose 90%.

5) Click on **Compute Interval.**

6) The following results are displayed.

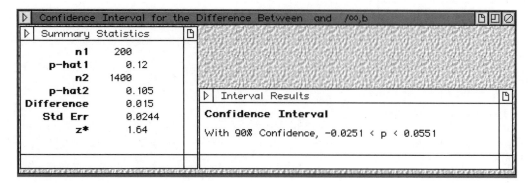

TO PRACTICE THESE SKILLS

You can practice the technology skills covered in this section by working on the following problems found in your textbook.

1) Work on problems 5, 7, and 9 in the Basic Skills and Concepts for Section 8-2 of your textbook. These problems focus on hypothesis testing and clearly identify the number of successes and trials for each sample.

2) Work on problems 21 and 24 in the Basic Skills and Concepts for Section 8-2 of your textbook. These problems focus on determining confidence interval estimates and require you to determine the number of successes for each sample.

3) Use Data Set 1 found in Appendix B or in the data file FHEALTH.xls to work through problem 30 in the Basic Skills and Concepts for Section 8-2 of your textbook.

SECTION 8-3: INFERENCES ABOUT TWO MEANS: INDEPENDENT SAMPLES

In this section we will work with sample data from two independent samples to test the hypothesis made about two population means. We will also construct confidence interval estimates of the differences between two population means. We will outline the following methods:

*   the Data Analysis **t-Test: Two-Sample Assuming Unequal Variances**

*   the DDXL add-in Hypothesis Tests: **2 Var t Test**

Enter the data found in Date Set 30 in Appendix B of your text or open the CD data file HOMERUN.xls to work through the **Hypothesis Test of Bonds and McGwire Homerun Distances** example found in Section 8-3 of your statistics book.

T-TEST: TWO-SAMPLE ASSUMING UNEQUAL VARIANCES:

1) Click on **Tools,** highlight **Data Analysis** and click.

2) From the Analysis Tools list box in the Data Analysis dialog box select **t-Test: Two-Sample Assuming Unequal Variances**.

3) Click on **OK.**

4) In the **t-Test: Two-Sample Assuming Unequal Variances** dialog box enter the following information:

a) Homerun distances for McGwire in the **Variable 1 Range** box.

b) Homerun distances for Bonds in the **Variable 2 Range** box.

c) You can enter 0 in the **Hypothesized Mean Difference** box or just leave it blank.

d) Enter 0.05 in the **Alpha** box. This value is supplied in the problem.

e) Determine where you wish to display the output.

f) Click **OK**.

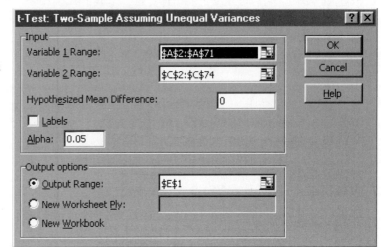

5) The following summary of information containing calculations for the t-test is added to your current Excel worksheet.

t-Test: Two-Sample Assuming Unequal Variances

	Variable 1	Variable 2
Mean	418.5142857	403.6712329
Variance	2069.731677	938.6959665
Observations	70	73
Hypothesized Mean Difference	0	
df	120	
t Stat	2.278793205	
P(T<=t) one-tail	0.012223652	
t Critical one-tail	1.657649591	
P(T<=t) two-tail	0.024447304	
t Critical two-tail	1.979929038	

Because the test statistic (t Stat = 2.278793205) falls within the critical region (t Critical 1.979929038) we reject the null hypothesis.

Note:

It is worth mentioning that this chart is not a "live" chart so that any changes made to the original data at this point would require using the Data Analysis Tool a second time to produce new test results.

DDXL – 2 VAR T TEST

Copy the homerun distances for McGwire and Bonds to a new worksheet.

1) Click on **DDXL**, select **Hypothesis Tests** and **2 Var t Test**.

2) In the dialog box click on the pencil icon for the **1ˢᵗ Quantitative Variable** and enter the range of data for the homerun distances for McGwire as you did before. Then click on the pencil icon for the **2ⁿᵈ Quantitative Variable** and enter the range of data for the homerun distances for Bonds.

3) Click **OK**

4) Follow these steps in the **2 Sample t Test Setup** dialog box:

    a) **Step 1:** Select **2-sample.**
    b) **Step 2:** This step is optional so you can skip over it or set the difference at 0.
    c) **Step 3:** Set the significance level at 0.05.
    d) **Step 4:** Select the appropriate alternative hypothesis.
    e) **Step 5:** Click on **Compute**.

5) The results can be seen below. In addition to the Test Summary, DDXL also returns the mean and standard deviation of each variable and a conclusion to reject the null hypothesis.

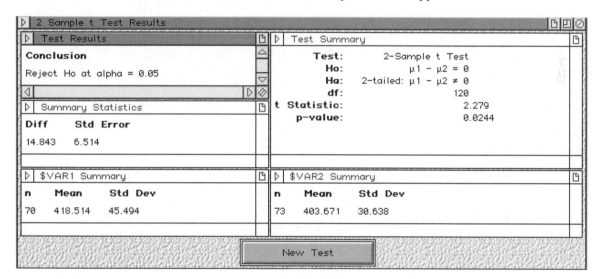

CONFIDENCE INTERVAL ESTIMATES

Using the sample data for **McGwire and Bonds** we can construct a confidence interval estimate of the difference between the mean homerun distance of McGwire and Bonds. This will be done using the DDXL add-in. The procedure for doing this is very similar to the one used to determine the 2 Var t Test.

1) Click on **DDXL**, select **Confidence Interval – 2 Var t Test.**

2) In the dialog box click on the pencil icon for the **1ˢᵗ Quantitative Variable** and enter the range of data for the homerun distances for McGwire as you did before. Then click on the pencil icon for the **2ⁿᵈ Quantitative Variable** and enter the range of data for the homerun distances for Bonds.

3) Click **OK**

4) In **2 Sample t Interval Setup**

    a) **Step 1:** Choose **2 sample**.
    b) **Step 2:** Select the appropriate confidence level (in this case 95%)
    c) **Step 3:** Click on **Compute Interval.**

5) The following results are displayed. In addition to the Confidence Interval results, DDXL also returns the mean and standard deviation for each variable.

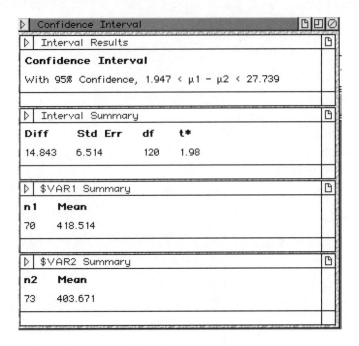

TO PRACTICE THESE SKILLS

You can practice the skills learned in this section by working through the following problems found in your textbook.

1) Use Data Set 17 found in Appendix B or in the data file COLA.xls to work through problem 11 in the Basic Skills and Concepts for Section 8-3 of your textbook.

2) Use Data Set 1 found in Appendix B or in the data file MHEALTH.xls to work through problem 23 in the Basic Skills and Concepts for Section 8-3 of your textbook.

SECTION 8-4: INFERENCES FROM MATCHED PAIRS

In the previous section we worked with independent populations. We now turn our attention to confidence interval estimates and hypothesis tests for dependent samples or matched pairs. The analysis can be done using either

- the Data Analysis **t-Test: Paired Two Samples for Means.**
- the DDXL add-in Hypothesis Tests: **Paired t Test**

Begin by entering the data found in Table 8–2 from the example **Are Forecast Temperatures Accurate?** into an Excel spreadsheet. This example is found in Section 8–4 of your textbook. Enter the data in columns rather than rows. The Data Analysis t Test requires that the data for each group be in a separate column. This is often referred to as **unstacked data**.

T-TEST: PAIRED TWO SAMPLES FOR MEANS

Using the data entered into Excel, we will test the claim that there is a difference between the actual low temperature and the low temperatures that were forecast five days earlier.

1) Click on **Tools,** highlight **Data Analysis** and click.

2) From the Analysis Tools list box in the Data Analysis dialog box select **t-Test: Paired Two Samples for Means.** Click **OK.**

3) In the t Test: Paired Two Samples for Means dialog box enter the following information

   a) The cell range containing actual lows in the **Variable 1 Range** box.
   b) The cell range for forecast lows in the **Variable 2 Range** box.
   c) Enter 0 in the Hypothesized Mean Difference box.
   d) Enter 0.05 in the **Alpha** box. This value is supplied in the problem.
   e) Determine where you wish to display the output.
   f) Click **OK.**

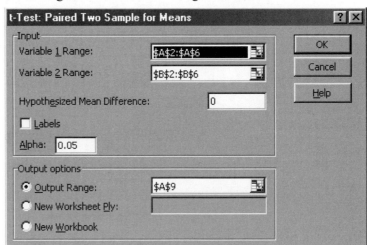

4) The following summary of information containing calculations for the t-test is in added to your current Excel worksheet.

t-Test: Paired Two Sample for Means		
	Variable 1	Variable 2
Mean	4.6	17.8
Variance	138.8	9.2
Observations	5	5
Pearson Correlation	0.4729313	
Hypothesized Mean Difference	0	
df	4	
t Stat	-2.762014037	
P(T<=t) one-tail	0.025372337	
t Critical one-tail	2.131846486	
P(T<=t) two-tail	0.050744673	
t Critical two-tail	2.776450856	

In addition to the test statistic, Excel displays the P values for a one and two tailed test as well as the corresponding critical values. These values can be compared with those found in Step 6 of the solution for the example **Are Forecast Temperatures Accurate?.**

You can also use DDXL to perform the hypothesis test for this problem.

DD

DDXL – PAIRED T TEST

1) Click on **DDXL** and choose **Hypotheses Tests** and **Pair t Test**.

2) In the Hypothesis test dialog box click on the pencil icon for the **1st Quantitative Variable** and enter the range of data for the actual lows. Click on the pencil icon for the **2nd Quantitative Variable** and enter the range of data for the forecast lows. Click on the pencil icon for the **Pair Labels** and enter the range of data for the difference between the actual lows and forecast lows.

3) Click **OK**.

4) In a manner very similar to the previous hypotheses tests done with DDXL complete the fours steps in the **paired t test** dialog box.

5) Click on **Compute**.

6) The following results will be displayed.

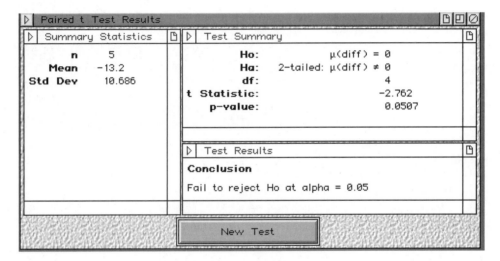

DDXL – CONFIDENCE INTERVALS FOR MATCHED PAIRS

Using the sample data from the preceding pages (Table 8–2) we can construct a confidence interval estimate of the mean of the differences between the actual low and the forecast low temperatures. This will be done using the DDXL add-in. The procedure for doing this is very similar to the one used to determine the 2 Var t Test.

1) Click on **DDXL**, select **Confidence Interval – Paired t Interval**.

2) In the dialog box click on the pencil icon for the **1st Quantitative Variable** and enter the range of data for the actual lows. Click on the pencil icon for the **2nd Quantitative Variable** and enter the range of data for the forecast lows. Click on the pencil icon for the **Pair Labels** and enter the range of data for the difference between the actual lows and forecast lows.

3) Click **OK**.

4) Select the appropriate confidence level (in this case 95%) and click on **Compute Interval.**

5)   The following results are displayed.

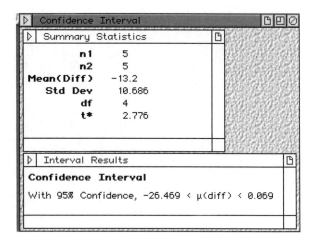

TO PRACTICE THESE SKILLS

Use the data presented in problems 5, 7 and 9 in the Basic Skills and Concepts for Section 8-4 of your textbook to practice the technology skills learned in this section.

SECTION 8-5: COMPARING VARIATION IN TWO SAMPLES

In this section we present a test of hypothesis for comparing two population variances. This will be done using the **F Test Two Sample for Variances** found in Excel's Data Analysis tools.

Open the file COLA.xls or enter the data found in Data Set 17 in Appendix B of your textbook. Determine the mean, variance and standard deviation using the weights of samples of regular Coke and regular Pepsi as seen below.

	regular coke	regular pepsi
mean	0.81682	0.82410
variance	0.000056	0.000033
standard deviation	0.007507	0.005701

Use this information and the **F Test Two Sample for Variance** found in Excel to work through the **Coke versus** Pepsi example found in Section 8-5 of your statistics book.

F-TEST: TWO SAMPLE FOR VARIANCES

Using the data entered into Excel, we will test the claim that the weights of samples of regular Coke and the weights of samples of regular Pepsi have the same standard deviation.

1)   Click on **Tools,** highlight **Data Analysis** and click.

2)   From the Analysis Tools list box in the Data Analysis dialog box select **F-Test Two Sample for Variances.**

3)   Click **OK**.

4) In the F- Test: Two Sample for Variances dialog box enter the following information:

a) The cell range containing the weight of regular Coke samples in the **Variable 1 Range** box.

b) The cell range for the weight of regular Pepsi in the **Variable 2 Range** box.

c) Since the range of cells in (a) and (b) did not include the labels for the columns leave this box unchecked. If you did include the labels check this box.

d) Enter 0.05 in the **Alpha** box. This value is supplied in the problem.

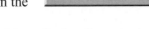

F-Test Two-Sample for Variances   ? ☒

Input
Variable 1 Range: $A$2:$A$37
Variable 2 Range: $B$2:$B$37

☐ Labels
Alpha: 0.05

Output options
⦿ Output Range: $D$6
○ New Worksheet Ply:
○ New Workbook

OK
Cancel
Help

e) Determine where you wish to display the output.

f) Click **OK**.

5) The following summary of information containing calculations for the F-test is in added to your current Excel worksheet.

F-Test Two-Sample for Variances		
	Variable 1	Variable 2
Mean	0.817	0.824
Variance	0.000	0.000
Observations	36.000	36.000
df	35.000	35.000
F	1.734	
P(F<=f) one-tail	0.054	
F Critical one-tail	1.757	

Excel will return the F test statistic, the P-value for the one-tailed case, and the critical F value for the one-tailed case. For a two-tailed test you can double the P-value returned by Excel.

TO PRACTICE THESE SKILLS

You can practice the technology skills learned in this section by working on the following problems found in your textbook.

1) Use Data Set 17 found in Appendix B or in the data file COLA.xls to work through problem 5 in the Basic Skills and Concepts for Section 8-5 of your textbook.

2) Use Data Set 20 found in Appendix B or in the data file CANS.xls to work through problem 6 in the Basic Skills and Concepts for Section 8-5 of your textbook.

3) Use Data Set 14 found in Appendix B or combine the data found in the files ROWLING.xls, and TOLSTOY.xls into a single worksheet in order to work through problem 15 in the Basic Skills and Concepts for Section 8-5 of your textbook.

CHAPTER 9: CORRELATION AND REGRESSION

SECTION 9-1: OVERVIEW

In this chapter we will be working with data that comes in pairs. We will be determining whether there is a relationship between the paired data, and will be trying to identify the relationship if it exists.

Excel provides an excellent tool to help us consider whether there is a statistically significant relationship between two variables. We can create a scatter plot, find a line of regression, and use our regression equation to predict values for one of the variables when we know values of the other variable.

The new functions introduced in this section are outlined below.

CORREL

This returns the correlation coefficient between two data sets. Your paired data must be entered in adjacent columns.

ADD TRENDLINE

This feature adds the linear regression graph to the scatter plot of a set of data values.

REGRESSION

This function returns information on Regression Statistics, as well as other information based on the linear regression equation. Your data values must be entered in adjacent columns.

SECTION 9-2: CORRELATION

In this section, we will take a look at a picture of a collection of paired sample data (boat/manatee) to help us determine if there appears to be a relationship between the variable x (number of registered boats) and the variable y (number of manatees killed by boats). We will work with the data from Table 9-1 in your textbook to learn how to create a scatter plot for the ordered pairs.

1) In cell A1, type in "Registered Boats." In cell B1, type in "Manatee Deaths."

2) Enter the paired data in column A and B, making sure that you keep the pairs as they are listed.

3) In cell C1, type" r =", and move your cursor to cell D1. To find the linear correlation coefficient, click on the **Function** icon on the main menu bar, or click on **Insert, Function.** In the **Category** box, click on **Statistical,** and in the **Function** box, select **CORREL.** Then click on **OK.**

4) In **Array1**, enter the range of cells where the data you want to use on your horizontal axis (x) is stored. In **Array2**, enter the range of cells where the data you want to use on your vertical axis (y) is stored. Then click on **OK**. You will see the correlation coefficient in cell D1. This value should round to 0.922. Read how we can interpret this value in the Example worked out in section 9-2 of your textbook.

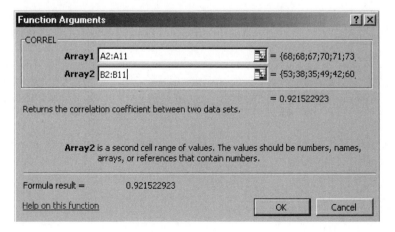

5) To create the scatterplot for this data, click on the **Chart Wizard** icon on the main menu, or click on **Insert, Chart.** Click on **XY(Scatter)**, and then click on **Next**.

6) In the **Data Range** box, enter the range of cells where your paired data is stored. If you entered your data in columns A and B starting with cell A2, you could type in "A2:B11". Make sure that the bullet by **Columns** is marked. Then click on **Next**.

7) Name your graph and your axes appropriately. You can also choose what other types of features you want to be included on your graph by accessing the tabs at the top of the **Chart Wizard** window. Click on **Next**.

8) Select the option of inserting your chart **As object in**: and select **Sheet 2**. Click on **Finish**.

9) Make appropriate adjustments to your chart size, font size, etc. to create a reasonable picture. Remember you can right click while your cursor is in any part of your chart to access formatting options for that particular region. For example, notice that there are no values shown which have an x coordinate less than 60, and a y coordinate less than 30, so eliminating that part of the graph is recommended. You can do this by right clicking on each of the axes, and then adjusting the scale. Your scatter plot should appear as the one shown below:

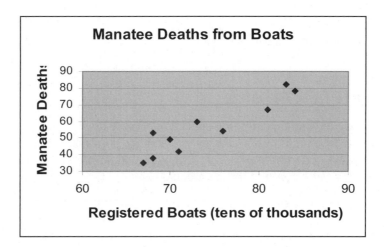

TO PRACTICE THESE SKILLS

You can apply the skills learned in this section by working on the following exercises.

1) Enter the data found in exercise 5 from Section 9-2 Basic Skills and Concepts in your textbook into Excel. Create the scatter plot, and find the linear correlation coefficient.

2) You can use Excel to work with exercises 15 through 24 from Section 9-2 Basic Skills and Concepts in your textbook. You can load the appropriate data from the CD that comes with your book. After you have loaded the data, you should copy the appropriate columns to a new worksheet. Create the scatter plot and find the linear correlation coefficient.

SECTION 9-3 & 9-4: REGRESSION, VARIATION AND PREDICTION INTERVALS

In section 9-2 we concluded that there was evidence of linear correlation between the number of registered boats and the number of manatee deaths from boats. Now we want to determine this relationship in order to be able to calculate the number of manatee deaths from boats once we know the number of registered boats.

We have two options when working with linear regression, both of which are outlined below.

- The first option (**Add Trendline**) allows us to quickly generate the line of regression directly from our scatter plot.

- The second option uses the data analysis feature, and gives us a much more information, which will be useful in considering a more thorough analysis of the situation.

Option 1 – Add Trendline

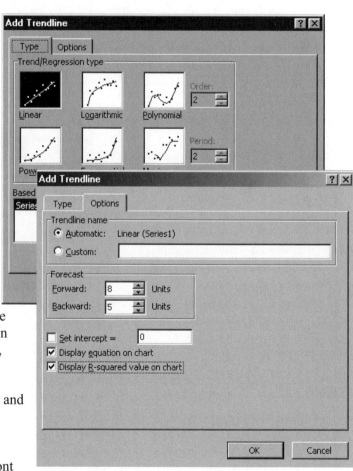

3) Click anywhere in the **Chart** region, and then click on **Chart** on the main menu. (Notice that until you click in the Chart region, Chart is not an option in the main menu line.) Select **Add Trendline**.

4) Make sure that **Linear** is selected from the possible types shown.

5) Click on the **Options** tab, and click in the box by **Display equation on chart**, and **Display R-squared value on chart**. Notice that there are options for Forecasting forward and backwards. Initially, the Trendline will automatically only include the beginning and ending output values from your data set. To extend the line to fill up more of the graph you can use the "Forecast" feature. In our example, we can go forward by 8 units, and backward by 5 units.

6) Click on **OK.** You will see your Trendline and the equation superimposed on your scatter plot.

7) You will probably want to reformat your font size for the equation, and reposition where the equation appears on the screen so that it does not cover any of your data points. You can do this by selecting the region containing the equation, then right clicking and selecting the "Format Data Labels" option. To move the equations, select the region containing the equation and move your cursor in this region until an arrow appears. Hold down the left click button, and move the box where you want it to be within your plot area.

8) You may find that when you used the forecast feature, your original scaling on your scatter plot changed. You can make additional changes if desired by double clicking on the axis that you want to adjust, selecting the tab labeled **Scale,** and making appropriate changes in the menu that appears.

9) Your picture should look similar to the one shown below. Notice that the equation shown does round off to the same equation that is shown in your book if you only wanted to use 3 significant digits for the slope and y intercept.

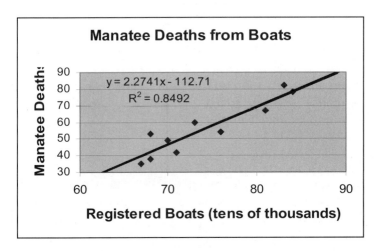

Option 2 – Data Analysis: Regression

1) Click on **Tools** from the main menu, then click on **Data Analysis**, and click on **Regression.** Click on **OK**.

2) Complete the **Regression** dialog box as shown. The cell addresses shown assume that you entered your x value label in cell A1, and your x values (Registered Boats) in cells A2 through A11. Your y value label is in cell B1, and your y values (Manatee Deaths) are in cells B2 through B11. If your data is entered in other cells, you should make appropriate adjustments.

- You should select both the column labels and the data in order to get the most useful, appropriately labeled output in terms of the contextual problem. Notice that if you do include the column headings, you must

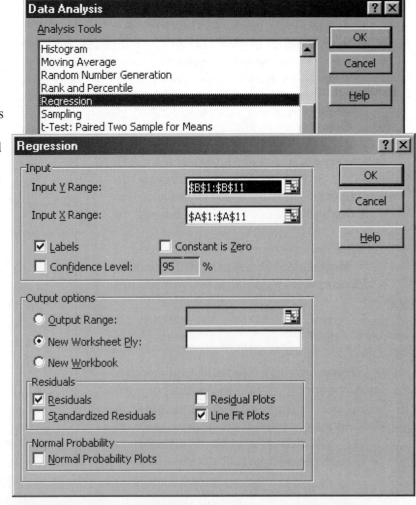

check the **Labels** box.   Otherwise Excel will give you an error message saying that you have selected non numeric data.

- You can either type in the cell addresses with a colon in between the beginning and ending cell, or you can select the cells in your worksheet.

- Notice, it is imperative that you are clear which data values represent your vertical (y) axis, and which data values represent your horizontal (x) axis.

3) Click on **OK**.

4) You will be taken to a new sheet, and will need to resize the columns to see all the information provided clearly. Remember, to do this you can click on **Format,** click on **Columns,** and then click on **AutoFit Selection**. You will see the information shown below.

SUMMARY OUTPUT

Regression Statistics	
Multiple R	0.921522923
R Square	0.849204498
Adjusted R Square	0.830355061
Standard Error	6.612348727
Observations	10

ANOVA

	df	SS	MS	F	Significance F
Regression	1	1969.814755	1969.814755	45.05198044	0.000150818
Residual	8	349.7852455	43.72315568		
Total	9	2319.6			

	Coefficients	Standard Error	t Stat	P-value	Lower 95%	Upper 95%
Intercept	-112.7098976	25.19240507	-4.473963374	0.00207231	-170.8037255	-54.61606976
Boats	2.274087687	0.338805353	6.712077207	0.000150818	1.492800637	3.055374737

RESIDUAL OUTPUT

Observation	Predicted Manatee Deaths	Residuals
1	41.92806511	11.07193489
2	41.92806511	-3.928065109
3	39.65397742	-4.653977422
4	46.47624048	2.523759517
5	48.75032817	-6.75032817
6	53.29850354	6.701496456
7	60.12076661	-6.120766605
8	71.49120504	-4.491205041
9	76.03938041	5.960619585
10	78.3134681	-0.313468102

5) You will also see a scatter plot showing both the actual data points as well as the points generated from the regression equation. You will need to resize and reformat this graph to make it look the way you want it to. You will also need to add the actual regression line. To add the line, double click on any one of the **Predicted** points. In the **Format Data Series** box that comes up, click in the bubble in front of **Automatic** under **Line**. (This can be found under the **Patterns** tab option.) You should create a picture similar to that shown below.

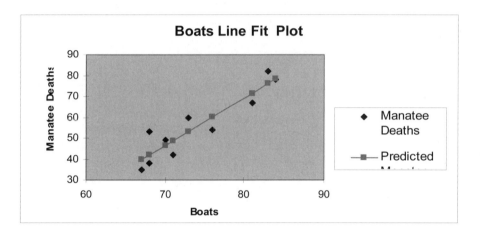

Interpreting This Output

Using the **Regression** option under **Data Analysis** provides you with more information than you need, but you can cut and paste the information that you need into another worksheet, or another document. To give you an idea of what the provided information represents, the major results are briefly described below:

- **Multiple R**: This is the correlation between the input variable (Boats) and the output variable (Manatee Deaths). Since for this example there is only one input, the value given here is the correlation coefficient, r, expressing the linear relationship between the number of boats and the number of manatee deaths.
- **R Square**: This is also referred to as the coefficient of determination. It represents the proportion of variation in the output that can be explained by its linear relationship with the input.
- **Adjusted R Square**: The sample R Square tends to be an optimistic estimate of the fit between the model and the real population. The adjusted R Square gives a better estimate.
- **Standard Error**: This is the standard error of the estimate, and can be interpreted as the average error in predicting the output by using the regression equation.
- **Observations**: This is the number of paired data values included in the analysis.
- **ANOVA**: You do not need to understand most of the information provided in this section for this chapter, but essentially this part of the output gives more detailed information about the variation in the output that is explained by the relationship with the input. For each source of variation, the output gives degrees of freedom (df), sum of squares (SS), the F value obtained by dividing the mean square (MS) regression by the mean square residual, and the significance of F, which is the P-value associated with the obtained value of F. A fuller treatment of the Analysis of Variance (ANOVA) can be found in chapter 11.
- **Coefficients**: These are the coefficients for your regression equation. The value listed in the first row is the y intercept of the regression line, while the value listed in the second row is the slope of the line.
- **T Stat**: This refers to a test of the hypotheses that the intercept is significantly different from zero.
- **P – Value:** This is the probability associated with the obtained t statistic.
- **Lower and Upper 95%:** These are the confidence interval boundaries for both the intercept and the slope.

- **Residuals:** This table shows you the values that would be predicted for the output when using the regression equation for each input value. The second column shows the difference between the predicted value and the actual data value.

TO PRACTICE THESE SKILLS

You can practice the skills learned in this section by working on the following exercises.

1) Open the workbook where you saved the data from exercise 5 in Section 9-2. Using this data, find the regression line utilizing both the **Trendline** option and the **Regression** option.

2) Open one or more of the workbooks where you saved the data from exercises 15 through 24 in Section 9-2 of your textbook. Using this data, find the regression lines and the other data using the **Regression** option for the paired data. Think about how you can use the information created under "Residual Output" to help you see whether there is a close linear relationship between the pairs of data values for each exercise. You can also use information generated in your tables to help you answer the questions asked for these exercises in Section 9-3 Basic Skills and Exercises in your textbook.

SECTION 9–5: MULTIPLE REGRESSION

The previous sections dealt with relationships between exactly two variables. This section presents a method for analyzing relationships that involve more than two variables. A multiple regression equation expresses a linear relationship between an output or dependent variable (y) and two or more inputs or independent variables (x values).

For this demonstration, we will use information on eight bears, as presented in Table 9-3 of your textbook. We will create an equation which expresses weight as the output (y) and head length and total overall length as the input variables (x values).

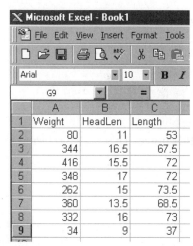

1) Enter the information given in Table 9-3 into a new Excel worksheet. **The values for the independent x values must be in adjacent columns**.

2) Click on **Tools, Data Analysis, Regression**.

3) Assuming that you have entered your data into the same cells as shown for this example, you would fill in the **Regression** dialog box with Y range being A1 to A9, and X range being B1 to C9.

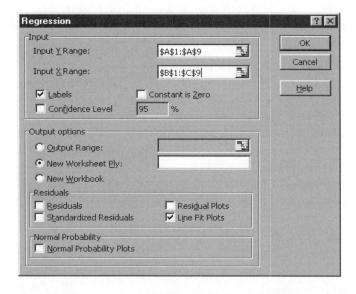

4) Click on **OK.**

5) You will see the information given below. From this information, you can create the equation: Weight = - 374 + 18.8(HeadLen) + 5.87(Length). For a discussion on other important elements, refer to the discussion in section 9-5 of your textbook.

SUMMARY
OUTPUT

Regression Statistics	
Multiple R	0.909935903
R Square	0.827983347
Adjusted R Square	0.759176686
Standard Error	68.56490584
Observations	8

ANOVA

	df	SS	MS	F	Significance F
Regression	2	113142.2684	56571.13422	12.03347661	0.012272308
Residual	5	23505.73157	4701.146313		
Total	7	136648			

	Coefficients	Standard Error	t Stat	P-value	Lower 95%
Intercept	-374.3034756	134.0930771	-2.791370619	0.03838268	-719.0001405
HeadLen	18.82040176	23.14805335	0.813044686	0.453152053	-40.68346649
Length	5.874757415	5.065488967	1.159761171	0.298513005	-7.146475235

TO PRACTICE THESE SKILLS

You can practice the skills learned in this section and in the previous section by working on exercises 9 through 12 from Section 9-5 Basic Skills and Concepts in your textbook.

SECTION 9-6: MODELING

We have used Excel to help us generate linear models for data sets. Although the **Regression** function does not give us the option to work with other types of models, we can generate scatter plots, and then add various types of Trendlines, including their equations. Your book shows various models that can be used with the TI-83 Plus calculator. In this section, we will use Excel to generate Quadratic, Exponential and Power models for the data set given in Table 9-5 of your book.

1) Enter the data for the Coded Year and the Population into a new worksheet.

2) To create the scatterplot for this data, click on the **Chart Wizard** icon on the main menu, or click on **Insert, Chart.** Click on **XY(Scatter)**, and then click on **Next.**

3) In the **Data Range** box, enter the range of cells where your paired data is stored. If you entered your data in columns A and B starting with cell

	A	B
1	Coded year	Population
2	1	5
3	2	10
4	3	17
5	4	31
6	5	50
7	6	76
8	7	106
9	8	132
10	9	179
11	10	227
12	11	281

A2, you could type in "A2:B12." Make sure that the bullet by **Columns** is marked. Then click on **Next**.

4) Name your graph and your axes appropriately. You can also choose what other types of features you want to be included on your graph by accessing the tabs at the top of the **Chart Wizard** window. Click on **Next**.

5) Select the option of inserting your chart **As object in**: and select **Sheet 2**. Click on **Finish**.

6) Make appropriate adjustments to your chart size, font size, etc. to create a reasonable picture. Remember you can right click while your cursor is in any part of your chart to access formatting options for that particular region.   Your scatter plot should appear as the one shown below:

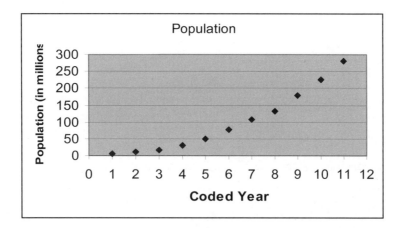

7) Click anywhere in the **Chart** region, and then click on **Chart** on the main menu. (Notice that until you click in the Chart region, Chart is not an option in the main menu line.) Select **Add Trendline**.

8) We will first find the Quadratic Model, so make sure that you have selected **Polynomial,** and that the **Order** is set at 2.

9) Click on the **Options** tab, and click in the box by **Display equation on chart**, and **Display R-squared value on chart**.

10) Click on **OK.** You will see your Trendline and the equation superimposed on your scatter plot.

11) You will probably want to reformat your font size for the equation, and reposition where the equation appears on the screen so that it does not cover any of your data points. You can do this by selecting the region containing the equation, then right clicking and selecting the "Format Data Labels" option. To move the equations, select the region containing the equation and move your cursor in this region until an arrow appears. Hold down the left click button, and move the box where you want it to be within your plot area. Your final picture should look like the one shown on the next page.

12) Notice that with appropriate rounding, the equation produced by Excel matches the one given in your textbook.

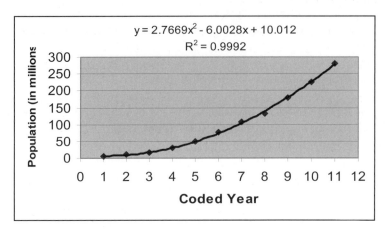

13) Suppose you wanted to now produce the exponential model for this same data set. You should first select the entire Chart Area by first clicking somewhere within the white region around your actual graph. You should then see the entire Chart Area "selected", and can then copy and paste the graph to another area of your worksheet so that you preserve the quadratic model. Once you have done this, you are ready to clear the quadratic Trendline from your scatter plot, and create an exponential model.

14) Make sure that your original Chart Area is **not selected**. You can click in any other cell in the worksheet to deselect the Chart Area. Then slowly move your cursor over your Trendline until you see the "yellow tag" appear which shows that you are pointing to the Trendline itself. Right click when you see this tag. You will see a box with 2 options: Format Trendline, or Clear. Select **Clear**. Your Trendline should then be removed from the picture, and you should be left with your original scatter plot.

15) Again, make sure that your Chart Area is selected so that you see the **Chart** option in the main menu line at the top of the page. Select **Chart**, and then select **Add Trendline.** Choose the **Exponential** option in the Add Trendline Dialog box. Then click on the **Options** tab, and make sure that you have checked off the options to display the equation and the r- squared value on the chart.

16) Click on **OK**.

17) After making some modifications to the graph, you should have a picture similar to the one shown below. Notice that the equation is not exactly the same as the one produced by the TI-83 Plus calculator. The calculator uses the exponential form y = a * b^x, whereas Excel uses the form a * e^ x. You may have

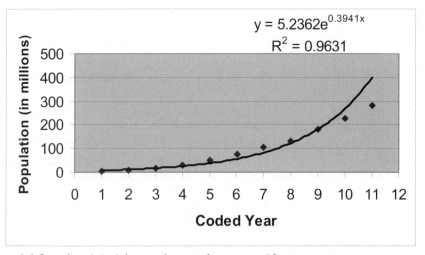

learned about the natural exponential function (e^x) in another math course. If you were to compute e raised to the numerical part of the power shown, you would find that the value produced is equivalent to the value for b shown in the TI-83 Plus screen. The two exponential models are equivalent ways to represent the equation that best fits the data.

18) Again, you should copy and paste this Chart Area to another part of your worksheet so that you can clear the Trendline from the original scatter plot, and use that Chart Area to create the third type of model, the Power Model. (Follow the previous steps 13 to 15 to clear the current Trendline.)

19) Again, make sure that your Chart Area is selected so that you see the **Chart** option in the main menu line at the top of the page. Select **Chart**, and then select **Add Trendline.** Choose the **Power** option in the Add Trendline Dialog box. Then click on the **Options** tab, and make sure that you have checked off the options to display the equation and the r- squared value on the chart.

20) After modifying your graph, you should have a picture similar to the one shown.

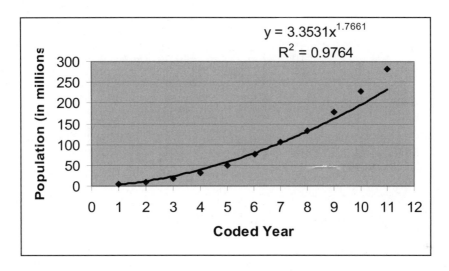

$$y = 3.3531x^{1.7661}$$
$$R^2 = 0.9764$$

21) Let's suppose that you now wanted to find out how closely your model matched the data given. We will work with the Power model, but you can follow similar procedures for any of the models. First find the Chart Area which contains the Power model and equations in your Excel worksheet. We recommend writing down the equation on a piece of paper so that you don't have to keep referring to the graph.

22) You need to input this expression in cell C2 in your worksheet, assuming that your first input value (coded year) is in cell A2 and your first output value (population in millions) is in cell B2. We need to modify this equation slightly so that Excel will understand that it is a formula. Make your modifications in the formula bar at the top of the screen. You need to insert the = sign before the expression so that Excel understands that it is a formula. You need to insert a * after the coefficient to indicate multiplication. To indicate that you want to use your natural exponential function, you would type EXP(, and then insert the exponent in parentheses. Your exponent needs to be adjusted by using a * after the numerical part, and then changing the x to a cell reference, in this case, cell A2. Your final formula bar should look as follows:

f_x =5.2362*EXP(0.3941*A2)

23) Once you have this formula entered correctly, press **Enter**. You should now see the value 7.76554 in cell C2.

24) You can now use the fill command to copy this formula down the rest of the column. Your table should look similar to the one below.

Coded year	Population	Predicted Values from Exponential Model
1	5	7.765540368
2	10	11.51667568
3	17	17.07979258
4	31	25.33016668
5	50	37.56587447
6	76	55.71202679
7	106	82.62365704
8	132	122.5349192
9	179	181.7252706
10	227	269.5074529
11	281	399.692717

25) You can follow similar procedures to create the predicted values for your quadratic model and your power model. The formulas you would need to input for each of these models are shown below.

Power Model: fx =3.3531*a2^1.7661

Quadratic Model: fx =2.7669*A2^2 - 6.0028*A2 + 10.012

26) You could now add other values into your Coded Year column, and continue to copy the formula for the predicted value down to include those input values.

TO PRACTICE THESE SKILLS

You can practice these skills by working on exercises 1 through 8 from Section 9-6 Basic Skills and Concepts in your textbook.

CHAPTER 10: MULTINOMIAL EXPERIMENTS AND CONTINGENCY TABLES

SECTION 10-1: OVERVIEW

In earlier chapters you learned that the first step in organizing and summarizing data for a single variable was to create a frequency table. It is often advantageous to categorize data and create frequency counts for different variables. It is also desirable to label data according to two quantitative variables for the purpose of determining whether or not these variables are related. This data is organized by using a **contingency table** (or two-way frequency tables). You have already learned the basics for creating tables in Excel by using the **Pivot Table** wizard introduced in Chapter 3. We will look at the Chi Square test for Independence, used to determine whether a contingency table's row variable is independent of its column variable.

CHITEST: returns the test for independence: the value from the chi-squared distribution for the statistic and the appropriate degrees of freedom.

CHITEST (actual_range, expected_range) where the actual_range is the range of data that contains observations to test against expected values and the expected_range is the range of data that contains the ratio of the product of row totals and column totals to the grand total.

SECTION 10 - 2: MULTINOMIAL EXPERIMENTS: GOODNESS-OF-FIT

In previous chapters you looked at several different hypothesis tests that assumed that the data came from a normally distributed population. There are other less formal ways to check to see if a population is normally distributed. These might include creating a histogram and observing if the shape resembles a normal distribution. While this is not a bad approach, we will feel more secure about decisions we make if we can substantiate our findings with a formal statistical technique. A **goodness-of-fit test** is one such technique.

Excel does not contain a built in function that will perform a goodness-to-fit test. Much of the work presented in this section can be done using the traditional paper and pencil approach. However, the use of technology makes the computational aspect of these problems much easier. By entering a formula in a cell and then copying that formula throughout the appropriate cells, it is possible to save time and avoid arithmetic mistakes. Keep this in mind when working through problems for Section 10-2 in your statistics textbook.

TO PRACTICE THESE SKILLS

You can practice the skills covered in this section by working through the following problem.

1) Use Data Set 26 found in Appendix B or in the data file LOTTO.xls to work through problem 13 in the Basic Skills and Concepts for Section 10-2 of your textbook.

SECTION 10-3: CONTIGENCY TABLES: INDEPENDENCE AND HOMOGENEITY

Excel provides the tools necessary to do a chi-square test for independence, although they are not found within a single analysis tool. The process involves (1) creating a contingency table using the **Pivot table** command in Excel, (2) determining the observed frequencies, (3) determining the expected frequencies and (4) using the **CHITEST** function.

The contingency table is the backbone of the chi-square test for independence in Excel.

Enter the information presented in Table 10-5 into Excel. This table represents the survival figures of the passengers of the Titanic.

	A	B	C	D	E	F
1		MEN	WOMEN	BOYS	GIRLS	**TOTAL**
2	SURVIVED	332	318	29	27	**706**
3	DIED	1360	104	35	18	**1517**
4	**TOTAL**	**1692**	**422**	**64**	**45**	**2223**

CREATING A TABLE OF EXPECTED FREQUENCIES

The contingency table provides the actual frequencies for each cell. To perform the chi-squared test for independence we also need the expected frequencies. Excel will expect to find these expected frequencies in a separate table and not within the table you just created.

1) Begin by copying the row headings (Men, Women, Boys, Girls) and column headings (Survived, Died) to a different location within the same Excel worksheet. We will use this new table for the expected frequencies.

2) Find the **expected frequency** for each cell in the new table created in step (1), using the formula

$$\text{expected frequencies} = \frac{(row\ total)(column\ total)}{grand\ total}$$ and the appropriate cell addresses.

Note:

You must use relative and absolute references if you are going to copy your formula to all of your cells and not just retype them in. If you have forgotten how to use relative and absolute references see Chapter 1, Section 1-6, for help.

---

3) If all is done properly you should see

	MEN	WOMEN	BOYS	GIRLS
SURVIVED	537.360	134.022	20.326	14.291
DIED	1154.640	287.978	43.674	30.709

PERFORMING THE CHI-SQUARE TEST

To test the hypothesis presented in the **Titanic Sinking** example found in Section 10-3 of your textbook we will use the statistical function **CHITEST** and perform the chi-square test. This function asks for the observed and expected values and will return the p value of the test.

1) Click on **Insert**, highlight **Function** and click.

2) From the **Paste Function Dialog box** highlight **Statistical** and then highlight **CHITEST.**

3) Click **OK.**

4) The **CHITEST** dialog box opens as shown below.

a) For the **Actual_range** highlight those cells that contain the observed frequencies (found in the first table we created). Be careful not to highlight the row and column totals.

b) For the **Expected_range** highlight those cells that contain the expected frequencies (found in the second table we created).

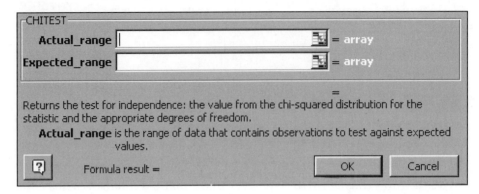

5) Click **OK.**

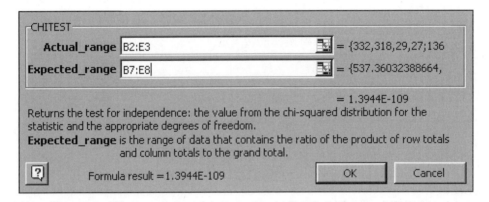

This returns a very small P-value. On the basis of this small P-value, we reject the null hypothesis and conclude that there is sufficient evidence to warrant the rejection of the null hypothesis of independence. Therefore we reject the hypothesis that whether a person survived the sinking of the Titanic is independent of whether the person is a man, woman, boy or girl.

TO PRACTICE THESE SKILLS

You can practice the skills presented in this section by working through problems 1, 5, 9 and 13 found in the Basic Skills and Concepts for Section 10-3 of your textbook.

CHAPTER 11: ANALYSIS OF VARIANCE

SECTION 11-1: OVERVIEW

In this chapter, we consider a procedure for testing the hypothesis that three or more means are equal. We will use the Analysis of variance (ANOVA) features of Excel.

Excel tools introduced in this section are outlined below.

ANOVA SINGLE FACTOR

This feature returns summary statistics on the data, as well as Analysis of Variance information.

ANAOVA: TWO FACTORS WITH REPLICATION

This feature returns summary statistics for each group in your data set, as well as Analysis of Variance information.

SECTION 11–2: ONE-WAY ANOVA

1) Open the three Excel files from the CD that comes with your book labeled CLANCY.XLS, ROWLING.XLS and TOLSTOY.XLS. Also open a new workbook where you will consolidate some of the information contained in your three files.

2) In your new worksheet, type in column headings of Clancy, Rowling and Tolstoy in cells A1, B1, and C1 respectively. Then copy the scores in the column for Flesch Reading Ease in the Clancy worksheet into cells A2 through A13. Copy the scores in the column for Flesch Reading Ease in the Rowling worksheet into cells B2 through B13. Finally copy the scores in the column for Flesch Reading Ease in the Tolstoy worksheet into cells C2 through C13. Your new worksheet should look like the one shown.

	A	B	C
1	Clancy	Rowling	Tolstoy
2	58.2	85.3	69.4
3	73.4	84.3	64.2
4	73.1	79.5	71.4
5	64.4	82.5	71.6
6	72.7	80.2	68.5
7	89.2	84.6	51.9
8	43.9	79.2	72.2
9	76.3	70.9	74.4
10	76.4	78.6	52.8
11	78.9	86.2	58.4
12	69.4	74.0	65.4
13	72.9	83.7	73.6

3) Click on **Tools** and click on **Data Analysis.** Click on ANOVA: **Single Factor**, and click on **OK.**

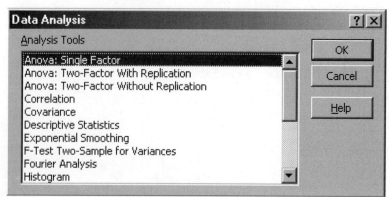

4) In the dialog box, type in "$A$1:$C$13" in the **Input Range,** or select these cells in your worksheet. Make sure that **Columns** and **Labels in First Row** are selected, and that **Alpha** is set at 0.05. You should have your results appear in a new worksheet. Then click on **OK**.

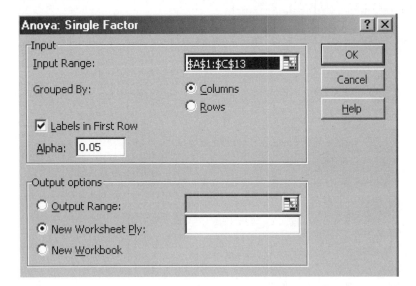

5) You will see a table of values that is automatically selected. Click on **Format, Column**, and click on **AutoFit Selection**.

6) You will see the table below.

ANOVA: Single Factor

SUMMARY

Groups	Count	Sum	Average	Variance
Clancy	12	848.8	70.73333333	128.2806061
Rowling	12	969	80.75	21.91545455
Tolstoy	12	793.8	66.15	61.74818182

ANOVA

Source of Variation	SS	df	MS	F	P-value	F crit
Between Groups	1338.002222	2	669.0011111	9.469487401	0.000562133	3.284924333
Within Groups	2331.386667	33	70.64808081			
Total	3669.388889	35				

7) For a discussion of the key components of this information, read through the material presented in section 11-2 of your textbook.

TO PRACTICE THESE SKILLS

You can practice the skills learned in this section by working on exercises 5 through 12 from Section 11-2 Basic Skills and Concepts in your textbook.

SECTION 11-3: TWO WAY ANOVA

For this demonstration, we will use the information presented in Table 11–4 of your textbook. You **MUST** enter the information for each age group of females and males down a column, not across a row, and each row must begin with the category of male or female.

1) Enter the data in Excel as shown below.

	A	B	C	D
1		21 - 29	30 - 39	40 and ove
2	male	13615	14677	14528
3	male	18784	16090	17034
4	male	14256	14086	14935
5	male	10905	16461	14996
6	male	12077	20808	22146
7	female	16401	15357	17260
8	female	14216	16771	25399
9	female	15402	15036	18647
10	female	15326	16297	15077
11	female	12047	17636	25898

2) Click on **Tools, Data Analysis,** and then click on **ANOVA: Two-Factor with Replication**. Click on **OK**.

3) Type in "$A$1:$D$11" in the box for **Input Range,** or select these cells in your worksheet. Type in 5 for **Rows per sample,** since you have 5 values for males and 5 values for females for each of the age groups. Type in 0.05 for **Alpha**. You should have your results appear in a new worksheet. Click on **OK**.

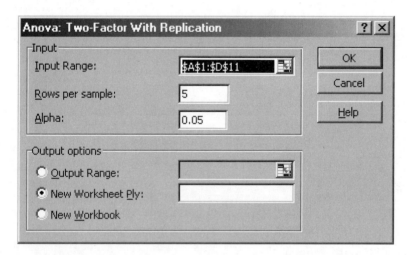

4) You will need to format the columns so that the titles all show up fully. You will see the data that is presented on the next page. For a detailed discussion of the values in this table, see section 11-3 in your textbook.

ANOVA: Two-Factor With
Replication

SUMMARY	21 - 29	30 - 39	40 and over	Total
male				
Count	5	5	5	15
Sum	69637	82122	83639	235398
Average	13927.4	16424.4	16727.8	15693.2
Variance	9087754.3	6962658.3	10125758.2	9165727.46
female				
Count	5	5	5	15
Sum	73392	81097	102281	256770
Average	14678.4	16219.4	20456.2	17118
Variance	2762103.3	1115302.3	24117287.7	14392308.6
Total				
Count	10	10	10	
Sum	143029	163219	185920	
Average	14302.9	16321.9	18592	
Variance	5423270.3	3601878.3	19080511.1	

ANOVA

Source of Variation	SS	df	MS	F	P-value	F crit
Sample	15225413	1	15225412.8	1.68637658	0.206419023	4.259675279
Columns	92086979	2	46043489.7	5.09980675	0.014265287	3.402831794
Interaction	21042069	2	10521034.3	1.16531657	0.32885108	3.402831794
Within	216683456	24	9028477.35			
Total	345037917	29				

TO PRACTICE THESE SKILLS

You can practice the skills learned in this section by completing exercises 13 and 14 from Section 11-3 Basic Skills and Concepts in your textbook. Remember, when working with exercise 13, you **MUST** enter the data for each age group in columns, with male or female beginning each row.

CHAPTER 12: NONPARAMETRIC STATISTICS

SECTION 12-1: OVERVIEW

In this chapter, many of the non-parametric methods used are not immediately supported by Excel. There are, however, some places where Excel can be used to help generate some of the intermediate steps in processes outlined in the sections.

The new functions we will use in this section are outlined below.

SIGN
This function determines the sign of a number. It returns 1 if the number is positive, zero (0) if the number is 0, and -1 if the number is negative.

COUNTA
This function counts the number of cells that are not empty and the values within the list of arguments. Use COUNTA to count the number of cells that contain data in a range or array.

COUNTIF
This function counts the number of cells within a range that meet the given criteria.

ABS
This function returns the absolute value of a number. The absolute value of a number is the number without its sign.

RANK
This function returns the rank of a number in a list of numbers. The rank of a number is its size relative to other values in a list. (If you were to sort the list, the rank of the number would be its position.)

SUMIF
This function adds the cells specified by a given criteria.

SECTION 12-2: SIGN TEST

We will use Excel where possible to help us organize the information that we need to use in conducting the Sign Test. The steps outlined below would be particularly beneficial if you were working with a large data set. With a small data set, you can probably do all the work as quickly by hand, however continuing to use Excel when possible allows you to continue building proficiency with the program.

1) Enter the data from Table 12-2 in your textbook into a new Excel worksheet. You should enter the data in columns as shown.

2) To use the Sign Test, we want to convert the raw data to plus and minus signs. We can use Excel to help us with this process by first creating a formula which subtracts the pairs, then using the

	A	B	C
1	Child	First Trial	Second Trial
2	A	30	30
3	B	19	6
4	C	19	14
5	D	23	8
6	E	29	14
7	F	178	52
8	G	42	14
9	H	20	22
10	I	12	17
11	J	39	8
12	K	14	11
13	L	81	30
14	M	17	14
15	N	31	17
16	O	52	15

SIGN function to give us a column representing the sign of the difference, and finally using the

COUNTA function to determine how many of the values are positive or negative. To accomplish this, follow the steps below.

3) In cell D2, enter the formula: =B2-C2. This will take the first trial value and subtract the second trial value from it. Then use the fill command to copy this formula down the rest of the column.

4) In cell E2, click on **Insert, Function.** In the **Category** box, click on **All,** and in the **Function** box, click on **SIGN.** Then click on **OK.**

5) In the dialog box that comes up, in the box after **Number,** type in D2 to indicate that the number you want to determine the sign for is in cell D2. Note that if the number is positive, the value returned will be 1. If the number is zero, the value returned will be 0. If the number is negative, the value returned will be -1. Click on **OK.**

6) Using the fill handle, copy this formula down the rest of the column. Your worksheet should now look similar to the one shown below.

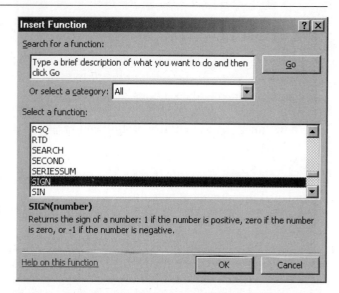

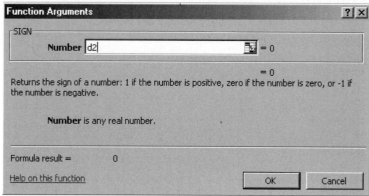

Child	First Trial	Second Trial	Differences	Sign
A	30	30	0	0
B	19	6	13	1
C	19	14	5	1
D	23	8	15	1
E	29	14	15	1
F	178	52	126	1
G	42	14	28	1
H	20	22	-2	-1
I	12	17	-5	-1
J	39	8	31	1
K	14	11	3	1
L	81	30	51	1
M	17	14	3	1
N	31	17	14	1
O	52	15	37	1

7) We now want to create a count of how many positive and how many negative values are contained in the sign column. Because this data set is small, it is easy to count the values, but we will still show how you can accomplish this with Excel so that you have tools which would make your work with a larger data set easier. In cell G2, type Positive, and in cell G3 type Negative.

8) Move to cell H2, and either click on the **Function** icon, or select **Insert, Function.** In the **Category** box, select **All.** In the **Function** box, select **Countif.** Then click on **OK.**

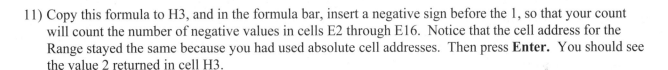

9) In the **Range** box, either enter $E$2:$E$16. These are the cells where our **SIGN** values are located in the worksheet. Since we will be copying this formula for the next count, it is essential that you use an absolute address.

10) Since we want to first find how many positive values there are, and since the positive values are indicated by 1, enter 1 in the **Criteria** box. Then click on **OK.** You should see the value 12 returned in cell H2.

11) Copy this formula to H3, and in the formula bar, insert a negative sign before the 1, so that your count will count the number of negative values in cells E2 through E16. Notice that the cell address for the Range stayed the same because you had used absolute cell addresses. Then press **Enter.** You should see the value 2 returned in cell H3.

TO PRACTICE THESE SKILLS

1) You can practice these skills by working on exercises 5 and 6 from Section 12-2 Basic Skills and Concepts in your textbook. You would enter the data for reported height and measured height in adjacent columns. After creating your number of positive and negative values, follow the procedures outlined in your textbook to complete the hypothesis test.

2) You can work on exercises 7 and 8, as well as exercises 11 through 13 from Section 12-2 Basic Skills and Concepts in your textbook. In these exercises, you would enter the given data in the first column, and fill the next adjacent column with the particular median value given in the particular exercise. Again, after creating your number of positive and negative values, follow the procedures outlined in your textbook to complete the hypothesis test.

SECTION 12-3 WILCOXON SIGNED-RANKS TEST FOR MATCHED PAIRS

Again, although Excel is not programmed for the Wilcoxon signed-ranks test, we can use Excel to help us complete some of the intermediate steps, particularly if the data set is large. We will use the data from Table 12-3 in your textbook to show you how and where Excel could be used to help produce information needed in order to perform the Wilcoxon signed-ranks test.

1) Follow steps 1 – 3 from section 12-2 of this manual to produce the worksheet shown, or copy the appropriate columns if you saved your work from the previous section to a new worksheet.

	A	B	C	D
1	Child	First Trial	Second Trial	Differences
2	A	30	30	0
3	B	19	6	13
4	C	19	14	5
5	D	23	8	15
6	E	29	14	15
7	F	178	52	126
8	G	42	14	28
9	H	20	22	-2
10	I	12	17	-5
11	J	39	8	31
12	K	14	11	3
13	L	81	30	51
14	M	17	14	3
15	N	31	17	14
16	O	52	15	37

2) Step 1 in your textbook for the Wilcoxon Signed-Ranks Procedure tells us to discard any pairs for which the difference is = 0. The easiest way to proceed is to select any row where the difference is zero, select **Edit** from the main menu bar, and then select **Delete**. For the data shown, we would only have to delete the first row.

3) Step 2 of the procedure tells us to ignore the signs of the differences and sort the differences from lowest to highest. To quickly create a column where we only show positive values, we can access the **ABS** function in Excel. In the column next to the difference column, position your cursor next to the cell which shows the first difference. Select **Insert Function**, and in the **Category** box, select **All**. In the **Function** box, select **ABS**. Press **OK**. In the **Number** box, type in the cell where your first difference appears. Then click on **OK**. Use your fill command to copy this formula down the rest of the column.

4) We now want to sort these values. Click on the letter at the top of the column containing the values that you want to sort to select that entire column. Then press the **Sort Ascending Icon.** A Sort Warning Box will appear, giving you the option to expand the current selection, or to continue with the current selection. Since we would like to keep the associated data with the sorted list, make sure that you choose the option to "Expand the Current Selection." When you press **OK**, you will see that the entire table of values is sorted along with the last column.

5) We now need to rank the differences. In the adjacent column, position your cursor in the cell next to the first sorted value. Select **Insert, Function**, and in the **Category** box, select **All**. In the **Function** box, select **Rank.** Fill in the dialog box as shown (or make adjustments where appropriate depending on where your data is located.) Make sure

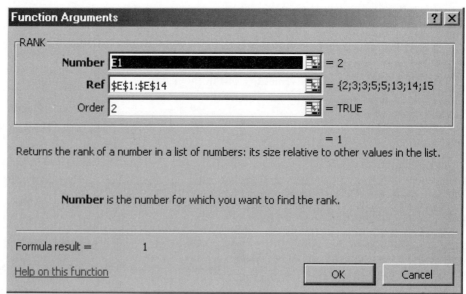

that the array shown in the **Ref** box is typed in using absolute addresses. In the **Order** box, you can type in any non zero number since the list of data is in ascending order. Then click on **OK**.

6) Use the fill command to copy this formula down the rest of the column. Your worksheet should now appear similar to the one shown. Notice that the entire set of columns has been rearranged. This occurred when you ranked the column of absolute values in ascending order. The advantage of this is that you can still associate particular ranked values with the original data points. If you had ordered only the one column, you would have lost this association.

H	20	22	-2	2	1
K	14	11	3	3	2
M	17	14	3	3	2
C	19	14	5	5	4
I	12	17	-5	5	4
B	19	6	13	13	6
N	31	17	14	14	7
D	23	8	15	15	8
E	29	14	15	15	8
G	42	14	28	28	10
J	39	8	31	31	11
O	52	15	37	37	12
L	81	30	51	51	13
F	178	52	126	126	14
Child	First Trial	Second Trial	Differences		

7) According to step 2 of the procedures in your textbook, when two values have the same rank value, you need to assign to them the mean of the ranks involved in the tie. In step 3 of the procedures, you also want to attach to each rank the sign of the difference from which it came. Notice that there are 2 ranks of 2, 4 and 8. Since the 2's appear in the 2nd and 3rd positions, you will replace each of the 2's with 2.5. Since the 4's appear in the 4th and 5th positions, you will replace each of them with 4.5, and since the 8's appear in the 8th and 9th positions, you will replace each of them with 8.5. Additionally, you have to check the difference column to see if the associated difference was positive or negative. We recommend creating a new column showing the signed ranks, and at the same time, make appropriate adjustments for tied ranks. If you do this, your last column should now look like the one shown below.

-1
2.5
2.5
4.5
-4.5
6
7
8.5
8.5
10
11
12
13
14

8) You now want to find the sum of the absolute values of the negative ranks, as well as the sum of the positive ranks. To make this process easier, we recommend sorting the table again in ascending order based on your last signed rank column. If you do this, all of your negative values will appear first in the column, followed by your positive values. To sort according to this column, click the letter at the top of the signed rank column to select that entire column. Then click on the **Sort Ascending Icon** on your menu bar, or click on **Data, Sort**. Again, you want to expand your selection so that all associated values are kept together. When you are done, your entire table should look like the one shown below.

Child	First Trial	Second Trial	Differences	ABS(Difference)	Initial Rank	Signed Rank
I	12	17	-5	5	4	-4.5
H	20	22	-2	2	1	-1
K	14	11	3	3	2	2.5
M	17	14	3	3	2	2.5
C	19	14	5	5	4	4.5
B	19	6	13	13	6	6
N	31	17	14	14	7	7
D	23	8	15	15	8	8.5
E	29	14	15	15	8	8.5
G	42	14	28	28	10	10
J	39	8	31	31	11	11
O	52	15	37	37	12	12
L	81	30	51	51	13	13
F	178	52	126	126	14	14

9) To find the sum of the negative ranks, click in a cell near your table, and select **Insert, Function, SUMIF.** Fill in the SUMIF dialog box as shown, making any appropriate adjustments to cell addresses if your signed ranks are in cells different than G1 through G14. Notice that you should use absolute cell addresses so that you can copy the formula and still

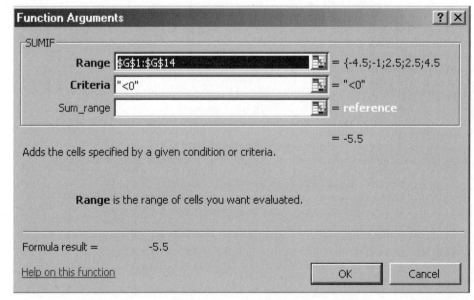

maintain the full range of ranks. In the Criteria box, type in < 0 to indicate that you want to sum up only the negative values in the given range of cells. You do not have to fill in the Sum_range box.

10) Copy your formula to the cell directly underneath it, and in the formula bar, change the < 0 to > 0 to indicate that we now want to sum up only the positive values in the range of cells. Then press **Enter.**

11) In your textbook, step 4 of the Wilcoxon Signed-Ranks Procedure says you want the sum of the absolute values of the negative ranks, so you need to make one further adjustment before you continue your work.

For the sum of the negative ranks, you should have gotten the value -5.5. You will want to adjust this to 5.5 when you go further with the test. You should have also found that the sum of your positive ranks was 99.5.

12) From this point on, continue to follow the steps outlined in your textbook to complete the hypothesis test.

TO PRACTICE THESE SKILLS

You can practice these skills by working on exercises 5 through 8 from Section 12-3 Basic Skills and Concepts in your textbook.

SECTION 12-4: WILCOXON RANK-SUM TEST FOR TWO INDEPENDENT SAMPLES

Although Excel is not programmed to compute the Wilcoxon Rank-Sum Test for Two Independent Samples directly, we can again make use of its features to help us obtain some of the information in the steps outlined in the procedure in section 12-4 of your textbook.

1) In a new worksheet, copy and paste the scores from the Flesch Reading Ease column from both the ROWLING and TOLSTOY Excel worksheets that are on the CD that comes with your book. You should paste the values into columns A and C, as you will want to leave room to insert the Rank in the adjacent column for each set of original data. Make sure you add the score of 71.4 to the Rowling scores, so that the data in your worksheet matches the data in Table 12-4 of your textbook.

2) Copy the values from each column and create a new column separate from the original data that combines the scores from both sets.

3) In the column next to your combined columns, beginning in the cell adjacent to the first score, insert the **Rank** function. Assuming that you begin your combined column in cell F1, your dialog box should be filled out as shown. (You may need to make adjustments if you created your combined column elsewhere in your worksheet. Notice

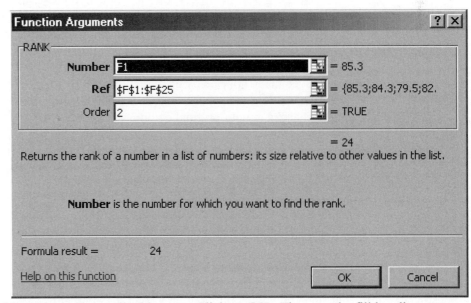

that the **Ref** box is filled in with absolute cell addresses. Click on **OK**. Then use the fill handle to copy the formula down the rest of the column. Your worksheet should now look like the one on the next page.

Rowling	Tolstoy	Combined Data	Rank
85.3	69.4	85.3	24
84.3	64.2	84.3	22
79.5	71.4	79.5	18
82.5	71.6	82.5	20
80.2	68.5	80.2	19
84.6	51.9	84.6	23
79.2	72.2	79.2	17
70.9	74.4	70.9	8
78.6	52.8	78.6	16
86.2	58.4	86.2	25
74	65.4	74	14
83.7	73.6	83.7	21
71.4		71.4	9
		69.4	7
		64.2	4
		71.4	9
		71.6	11
		68.5	6
		51.9	1
		72.2	12
		74.4	15
		52.8	2
		58.4	3
		65.4	5
		73.6	13

4) In order to see if there are any "repeating ranks", you should copy the rank column to another column in your worksheet, and then sort only that copied column. When you copy the column, you will need to use the **Paste Special** command, and paste the **Values** only. Since you want to be able to fill in the ranks for the values in each original column of data, you DO NOT want to rearrange the entire table of data as you did in the last section.

5) In the sorted column, notice that 9 appears twice, but all other ranks appear only once. Since the 9's appear in the 9th and 10th position, you would average 9 and 10, and then replace each rank of 9 with the value 9.5. Make these changes in your original column of combined data values.

6) Now select the ranks associated with the values in the top half of the table that came from your original Rowling column. Copy these values, and using the **Paste Special** command, paste the **Values** only in the column adjacent to the Rowling data. Copy and paste the ranks associated with the Tolstoy data into the column next to your original Tolstoy data.

7) Your table should now match Table 12-4 in your textbook.

8) You now want to compute the **Count** for each of your rank columns, as well as the **Sum.** In column A, type in Count and Sum below your data values. Then under the columns containing your ranked values, use your **Count** function and your **Sum** function to find the number of values in each column, as well as the sum of the rank values in each column. Your worksheet should look similar to the one shown on the next page.

Rowling		Tolstoy	
85.3	24	69.4	7
84.3	22	64.2	4
79.5	18	71.4	9.5
82.5	20	71.6	11
80.2	19	68.5	6
84.6	23	51.9	1
79.2	17	72.2	12
70.9	8	74.4	15
78.6	16	52.8	2
86.2	25	58.4	3
74	14	65.4	5
83.7	21	73.6	13
71.4	9.5		

Count	13	12
Sum	236.5	88.5

9) Although you can compute the mean and standard deviation of the sample R values using Excel, it is probably easier to do these computations using a calculator than to take the time entering the appropriate cell based formulas into Excel. Likewise, computing your test statistic is more simply done on a calculator.

10) Read the solution in your textbook to see how you use the values generated to make a decision in your hypothesis test.

TO PRACTICE THESE SKILLS

You can practice the skills learned in this section by working with exercises 3 through 10 from section 12-4 Basic Skills and Concepts in your textbook.

SECTION 12-5: KRUSKAL-WALLIS TEST

Again, Excel is not programmed to directly perform the Kruskal-Wallis Test. As in the previous section, you can use Excel to help you work through the preliminary work outlined in the procedures for performing the test in your textbook.

Since the only difference between this section and the previous section is that you are working with an additional column of data, we have chosen to just refer you back to section 12-4. You would be setting your initial data up in 3 columns, leaving a column between successive data values, so that you could copy in the ranked values once you find them. In a separate column, you would combine all of the data values, and then use the **Rank** function to find the Ranks for these values. Again, you would want to copy the ranked column, and order it so that it is easy to see if there are any repeated ranks. As before, you would replace the repeated ranks with the average value. Once you have changed the appropriate values in the original column of ranks, you would then copy and paste (using Paste Special Values) the associated ranks in the columns next to the original data. You can then use your **Count** and **Sum** functions to find the values for n and R. At that point, you would use these values in the formula for H shown in your textbook.

TO PRACTICE THESE SKILLS

To practice the skills outlined in this section, you can work on exercises 3 through 8 from Section 12-5 Basic Skills and Concepts in your textbook.

SECTION 12-6: RANK CORRELATION

We will use Excel to help us create the test statistic for the data shown in Table 12-7 of your textbook.

1)   In columns A and C of a new worksheet, type in the data for the Number of games played and the Score respectively.

2)   In column B, use the **Rank** function, making sure that your **Ref** box uses the absolute cell addresses for the range of cells in column A where your data is located.   Since you want your ranks to be computed for the data in ascending order, you should type in a non-zero value in the **Order** box.

3)   Use your fill handle to copy this formula down the rest of the column.

4)   Follow a similar pattern to create the ranks for the data for scores.

5)   To find the rank correlation coefficient for the paired ranked data values (found in columns B and D in the worksheet shown) we can use the **CORREL** function, using the range of cells containing values in column B as **Array 1**, and the range of cells containing values in column D as **Array 2**. Using this function with the columns shown below will produce a rank correlation coefficient of 0.95.

	A	B	C	D
1	Number of games	Rank for Number of games	Score	Rank for Scores
2	9	2	22	2
3	13	4	62	4
4	21	5	70	6
5	6	1	10	1
6	52	7	68	5
7	78	8	73	8
8	33	6	72	7
9	11	3	58	3
10	120	9	75	9

TO PRACTICE THESE SKILLS

You can practice the skills from this section by working on exercises 6 through 12 from Section 12-6 Basic Skills and Concepts in your textbook.

CHAPTER 13: STATISTICAL PROCESS CONTROL

SECTION 13–1: OVERVIEW

In this chapter, we address changing characteristics of data over time. In monitoring this characteristic, we are able to control the production of goods and services.

The major features used in this section are ones that have already been introduced in earlier sections, and include:

Chart Wizard to create a line graph from a set of data points.

Function used to access **Average, Median,** and **STDEV.**

The new feature introduced in this section is how to use the **Callouts** under the Draw menu.

SECTION 13–2: CONTROL CHARTS FOR VARIATION AND MEAN

In this section, we will consider data arranged according to some time sequence. We will consider the information on Aircraft Altimeter Errors (in feet) found in Table 13-1 in your textbook.

1) Enter the data for the day and the Aircraft Altimeter Errors in a new worksheet. You do not have to type in the data for the last four columns of the table shown in your textbook, as we can create these using Excel.

2) To create the columns for the mean, median, range and sample standard deviation for each row, click on the function icon, or click on **Insert, Function.** Then select **Statistical, Average (or Median, or STDEV).** Click on **OK**, and in the dialog box, enter cells B2 through E2 (the cells containing the actual aircraft altimeter errors for a given day). Press **Enter**. To create one decimal place for the Mean and Standard Deviation, click on **Format, Cells, Number**, and type in 1 for the number of decimal places you want to have shown. Use the fill handle to fill in the rest of the column. To create 2 decimal places for the Standard Deviation, follow the same procedures, but type in 2 for the number of decimal places you want to have shown.

3) To create the column for the Range, position your cursor in cell H2, and type in the formula: = Max(B2:H2)-Min(B2:H2). Press **Enter**. Use the fill handle to fill in the rest of the column.

4) You should now have the table shown on the next page.

Day					Mean	Median	Range	St.Dev
1	2	-8	5	11	2.5	3.5	19	7.94
2	-5	2	6	8	2.8	4.0	13	5.74
3	6	7	-1	-8	1.0	2.5	15	6.98
4	-5	5	-5	6	0.3	0.0	11	6.08
5	9	3	-2	-2	2.0	0.5	11	5.23
6	16	-10	-1	-8	-0.8	-4.5	26	11.81
7	13	-8	-7	2	0.0	-2.5	21	9.76
8	-5	-4	2	8	0.3	-1.0	13	6.02
9	7	13	-2	-13	1.3	2.5	26	11.32
10	15	7	19	1	10.5	11.0	18	8.06
11	12	12	10	9	10.8	11.0	3	1.50
12	11	9	11	20	12.8	11.0	11	4.92
13	18	15	23	28	21.0	20.5	13	5.72
14	6	32	4	10	13.0	8.0	28	12.91
15	16	-13	-9	19	3.3	3.5	32	16.58
16	8	17	0	13	9.5	10.5	17	7.33
17	13	3	6	13	8.8	9.5	10	5.06
18	38	-5	-5	5	8.3	0.0	43	20.39
19	18	12	25	-6	12.3	15.0	31	13.28
20	-27	23	7	36	9.8	15.0	63	27.22

Control Chart for Monitoring Variation: The R Chart

1) Before we create the actual chart for the ranges, we need to compute the value for the Centerline, and the values for the Upper Control Limit (UCL) and the Lower Control Limit (LCL).

2) To find the mean of the sample ranges, position your cursor in a cell under the column containing the sample ranges. Click on the **Function** icon, click on **Statistical** and **Average.** Select the cells containing the sample ranges, and then press **Enter.** You should find the mean of the sample ranges is 21.2.

3) To find the upper and lower control limits, we must use Table 13–2 in your textbook and locate the value for D_3 and D_4. Since the number of observations in each subgroup is 4, we look under the column for R, and find that the values we want are .000 and 2.282 respectively.

4) Compute the upper control limit using the following pattern: D_4 * (mean of the ranges). Your upper control limit will be $(2.282)(21.2) = 48.4$

5) Compute the lower control limit using the following pattern: D_3 * (mean of the ranges). Your lower control limit will be $(0.000)(21.2) = 0.00$.

6) We need to add these values to our table. Select the three columns **directly to the right** of the column containing your sample ranges by positioning your cursor on the column letter, holding the mouse down, and dragging over the other two columns so that all three are highlighted. Click on **Insert** and select

Columns. You should now have three blank columns inserted in your table directly to the right of the column of means.

7) At the top of the first blank column, type in "Mean of ranges." In the cell directly underneath this, type in the value you produced above of 21.2. Use the fill handle to fill in the remaining rows of this column with this value.

8) At the top of the next column, type LCL. In the cell directly underneath this, type in the value of your lower control limit, and fill the remaining table rows in this column. Repeat this procedure for the upper control limit in the third column you created.

9) Click on the **Chart Wizard** icon. For the **Chart type**, click on **Line**, and for the **Chart subtype**, click on the first graph in the second row. Then click on **Next**.

10) Make sure that the bubble by **Columns** is checked. For Data Range, select cells H2 through K21, since this is where your range data, mean of ranges and lower and upper class limits is contained. You will see =Sheet1!$H$2:$K$21 entered in the box by **Data Range**.

11) Click on the **Series** tab, and under the Series box, click on Series 1. Move your cursor to the **Name** box, and select the column title from your worksheet which represents the data for Series 1 (this should be your Range). Repeat this for each of the Series listed. You should see

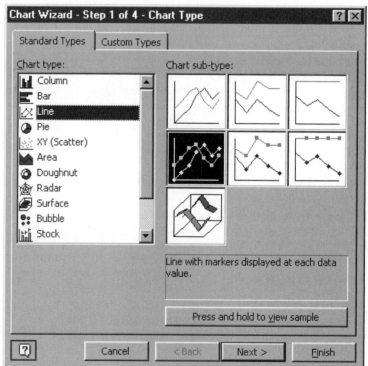

the names in the legend box change to represent the appropriate title for the data displayed. Then click on **Next.**

12) Fill in the **Chart Options** as shown. Then click on the **Gridlines** tab, and make sure that none of the options are selected. Then click on **Next**.

13) For **Chart Location**, select **As object in**, and choose **Sheet 2** from the drop down menu. Then click **Finish**.

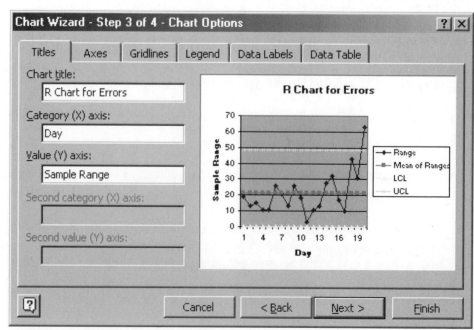

14) You should make appropriate adjustments to your graph so that it looks like the one shown below.

15) If you want to eliminate the markers on any of the horizontal lines, click on any one of the markers. In the **Format Data Series** dialog box, click in the bubble beside **None** in the column labeled **Markers.**

16) To add the information on the values for the horizontal lines, click on **AutoShapes** on the **Drawing Toolbar** at the bottom of your screen. (If the Drawing Toolbar is not available, click on **View,** select **Toolbars,** and from this menu, click in front of **Drawing.**)

17) Click on **Callouts**, and select the callout style of your choice. You can edit the font size, and move the box where you want it to be, as well as shifting the "handle". You should experiment with this option, as it provides an excellent way to add information to any graph.

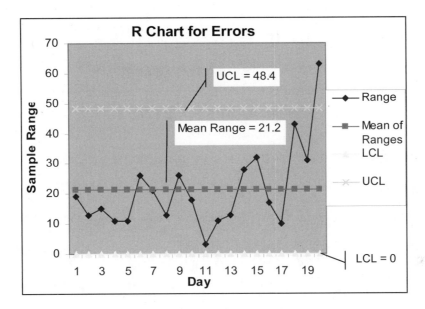

Control Chart for Monitoring Means

You can follow basically the same procedures as those above to create a chart for the sample means. The major differences are outlined below.

1) Your **Data Range** and **Chart Title** will need to reflect the fact that you are using the sample means, not the sample ranges

2) To find the upper and lower control limits, we must use Table 13–2 in your textbook and locate the value for A_2. Since the number of observations in each subgroup is 4, we look under the column for the mean, and find that A_2 is 0.729.

3) We will use the mean of the ranges that we found before. We also need to compute the mean of the sample means. To do this, you can copy the formula from the cell containing the mean of your sample ranges to a cell under the column showing the means. You should find that the mean of the sample means is 6.45.

4) Compute the upper control limit using the following pattern: Mean of sample means $+ A_2 *$ (mean of the ranges). Your upper control limit will be $6.45 + (.729)(21.2) = 21.9$

5) Compute the lower control limit using the following pattern: Mean of sample means + A_2 * (mean of the ranges). Your lower control limit will be $6.45 - (.729)(21.2) = -9.0$.

6) Again, we need to add these values to our table. Select the three columns **directly to the right** of the column containing your sample means by positioning your cursor on the column letter, holding the mouse down, and dragging over the other two columns so that all three are highlighted. Click on **Insert** and select **Columns.** You should now have three blank columns inserted in your table directly to the right of the column of means. At the top of the first blank column, type in "Mean of means". In the cell directly underneath this, type in the value you produced above of 6.45. Use the fill handle to fill in the remaining rows of this column with this value. At the top of the next column, type LCL. In the cell directly underneath this, type in the value of your lower control limit, and fill the remaining table rows in this column. Repeat this procedure for the upper control limit.

7) Your final graph should end up looking much like the one shown below. Again, you could add the values for your mean of the sample means, UCL and LCL by utilizing the **Callout** feature in the **AutoShapes** menu.

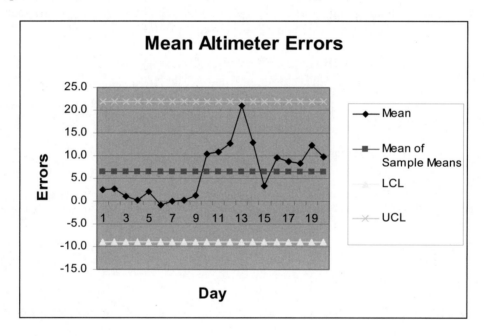

TO PRACTICE THESE SKILLS

You can apply the skills learned in this section by working on exercises 5, 6, 8, 9, 11 and 12 from Section 13-2 Basic Skills and Concepts in your textbook..

SECTION 13-3: CONTROL CHARTS FOR ATTRIBUTES

Whereas in section 13-2 we worked with quantitative data, this section works with qualitative data. We will again be selecting samples of size n at regular time intervals and plot points in a sequential graph with a centerline and control limits.

For illustration, we will work with the information on the example **Deaths from Infectious Diseases** in your textbook.

1) Enter the information on number of deaths in column A of a new worksheet.

2) You need to create a column showing the proportion of the sample that each number of deaths represents. Type "p" in cell B1. Position your cursor in cell B2. Since each year, 100000 people were selected, we will enter the formula: =A2/100000 and press **Enter.** You should see the value .00025 in cell B2. Copy this formula down through cell B14.

3) Since we need to find $\bar{p}$, we need to find the sum of the values in column A. Position your cursor in cell A16, and type in the word "sum". Move to cell A17, and select the **Summation** symbol on your toolbar. You will see the formula: = sum(A2:A16), and you will see that the cells A2 through A16 have been selected. Click to the right of the 6 within the parentheses, delete this number, and type in 4, since you only want to add from A2 through A14. Then click **Enter.** You should now see the value 375 listed.

4) To find $\bar{p}$, you need to divide this sum by the total number of subjects sampled. Since the example is for information obtained over 13 years, and 100,000 people were selected each year, you can create this value by creating the following formula in cell C2: = $A$17/(13*100000). In cell C1, name the column "p-bar". Then, since you are going to want to graph a horizontal line at this height on your graph, copy the value obtained from the formula (.000288) down through cell C14.

5) You now need to compute the upper control limit and the lower control limit. We will use the formulas found in your textbook. To find $\bar{q}$, position your cursor in cell C16 and type in the word "q-bar". Then move to cell C17 and enter the following formula: =1-$C$2. Then press **Enter.** You should see the value 0.999712 listed.

6) Type "LCL" in cell D1 of your worksheet, and enter the following formula in cell D2: =$C$2-3*SQRT($C$2*$C$17/(100000)). This utilizes the value for $\bar{p}$ and $\bar{q}$ which has previously been computed in your worksheet in cells C2 and C17 respectively. Notice that the cell addresses are absolute, meaning that they will not be updated as we copy the formula into different columns.

7) Type "UCL" in cell E1, and copy the formula from cell D2 into cell E2. Position your cursor in front of the minus sign in the formula bar, delete it, and type in +. Then press **Enter.** You should see the value .00045 in cell E2. Copy this formula down through cell E14.

8) When you are done with this work, you should have a table much like that shown on the next page.

# of Deaths	p	p-bar	LCL	UCL
25	0.00025	0.000288	0.000127	0.00045
24	0.00024	0.000288	0.000127	0.00045
22	0.00022	0.000288	0.000127	0.00045
25	0.00025	0.000288	0.000127	0.00045
27	0.00027	0.000288	0.000127	0.00045
30	0.0003	0.000288	0.000127	0.00045
31	0.00031	0.000288	0.000127	0.00045
30	0.0003	0.000288	0.000127	0.00045
33	0.00033	0.000288	0.000127	0.00045
32	0.00032	0.000288	0.000127	0.00045
33	0.00033	0.000288	0.000127	0.00045
32	0.00032	0.000288	0.000127	0.00045
31	0.00031	0.000288	0.000127	0.00045

Sum		q-bar
		0.999712
375		

9) Now use your **Chart Wizard**, and **Line** graph option to create the Control Chart. You will want to use a **Data Range** of cells B1 through E 14. Make sure that you deselect any gridline options. After modifying your graph as appropriate, you should end up with a picture similar to that shown below.

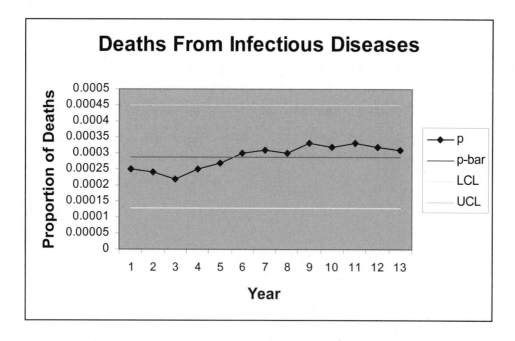

TO PRACTICE THESE SKILLS

You can apply the technology skills learned in this section by completing exercises 5, 6, 7 and 8 from Section 13-3 Basic Skills and Concepts in your textbook.